# THEIR
# WEB

# THEIR WEB

## THE LEFT'S WAR ON TRUTH

### ALEK DREXLER

LIBERTY HILL PUBLISHING

Liberty Hill Publishing
2301 Lucien Way #415
Maitland, FL 32751
407.339.4217
www.libertyhillpublishing.com

Paperback ISBN-13: 978-1-66283-520-9
Dust Jacket ISBN-13: 978-1-66283-521-6
Ebook ISBN-13: 978-1-66283-522-3

# DEDICATION

To my family, who supports me despite any differences we might have. To my mom, who, despite my flaws, continually does what's best for me. To the United States of America, thanks you for giving me a chance at being whatever I want to be.

# TABLE OF CONTENTS

"The radical view of American history is a web of lies, all perspective is removed, every virtue is obscured, every motive is twisted, every fact is distorted, and every flaw is magnified until the history is purged and the record is disfigured beyond all recognition. This movement is openly attacking the legacies of every person on Mount Rushmore. They defiled the memory of Washington, Jefferson, Lincoln, and Roosevelt. Today we will set history and history's record straight."

-Donald Trump,
Independence Day speech, July 3, 2020

# PART ONE

## TOOLS OF DESTRUCTION

---

THE ATROCITY WE NOW know as the Democratic Party has become something of a monster, a Frankenstein's monster of their own creation, sewn together with rotten chunks of lies and deceit, if you will. They are a terrorizing force, casting a shadow of doubt over the future of our beloved nation. They have done a pretty good job of reversing any progress that our country has made in the past century. The worst part about it is they have all the necessary resources they need to bring America to its knees. They control the FBI, the majority of news sources, social media, radical anti-American extremist groups, Hollywood, and even free speech. They have turned these into weapons of destruction, so in the first part of this book, I will pick apart how they have cracked and chipped away at the traditional values of American exceptionalism, from liberal hypocrites to the Democratic news' mass manipulation. I will attempt to cover all the major bases that make up the modern Democrat Party.

# 1.

# A Chance to be "Modest"

BY THE CHAPTER'S TITLE, I'm sure you're thinking,
"That's nice." And you'd be wrong to think that. I could tell you that
the Democratic Party isn't the only organization that lies. I could mention how the GOP isn't rock solid either. But I only said a *chance* to be
modest. I'm not going to be modest right now. In this chapter, I am
going to be honest and truthful, *not* modest. I'm as sure as heck not
going to be humble either. I'm going to tell you the hard truth. For years
now, the Democrats have spewed lies to try and gain your support. They
will make sure every lie they tell has a smaller lie to fill in any missing
details. They have, for decades, been doing this. You could *say* that they
have made an intricate web of lies.

Sure, the GOP has had a few bum breaks and a few crude presidents, to say the least. But the truth is we have an outstanding record
of progress. While the Republicans have put the American people first,
the Democrats have put their pride first. On multiple occasions, the
Democrats have refused to compromise or work with others with different political philosophies. For instance, on a regular basis, Nancy
Pelosi publicly mocked and insulted the former president and his ability

to lead. How many times did she try to impeach him? How is America going to grow if the political parties refuse to be civil? The answer: it can't.

Although I don't plan to make it a Republican vs. Democratic issue, I intend to make the American people against the Democrats' system of favoritism and oppression an issue. At times in this book, I will blame Democrats, in general. So if you don't have the stomach for insults, return this book to the shelf that it came from.

For far too long, the liberals have played the game of teacher's pet, and it has affected everyone. It is not just the people they choose to ignore that it hurts; it affects the nation's Democratic process and upsets the very principles of American exceptionalism. They are selective in who they choose to listen to and whom they deem too offensive to pay a lick of attention to.

To put it simply, they act like little kids. They try to enforce the rule every parent had for them when they were kids, "If you don't have anything nice to say, don't say it at all." So when they feel that someone has just broken that rule for them, they go running to the nearest media outlet that will listen and tattle. "Johnny said this! Julia believes that! Tell them that they can't say those things!" It's actually hilarious to watch! Their need to protect their fragile eggshell egos is worth so much more to them than being open to change. It is because the idea of change is scary. It's scary for all of us, but for them, it's like one of those *choose your own adventure* type books: make all the same "safe" decisions, and you won't have to be confronted with any "tough" demands. They refuse to take the road less traveled, and that, in itself, is more harmful than helpful. By condemning one person for their opinion, you condemn every other person who has the same views.

For years, the Dems have shown how much of a party of hypocrites they indeed are. They jump on the allegations a washed-up porn star makes about the Republican president as the gospel truth. But when a former secretary for Joe Biden comes forward with allegations of sexual harassment, they say that it's "disgusting" how someone could make up such blatant lies just to get attention. The very same party that backs the #MeToo movement attacks a woman with a serious allegation. I thought all voices needed to be heard? Now I'm not saying the claims are valid–because everyone is innocent until proven guilty–but for some reason, they can believe the craziest things about Trump but not the one rape allegation against Biden? Because any reasonable person would totally believe that a single man could have found the time to run several multi-million dollar businesses, get divorced, raise kids, go bankrupt several times, found a college, have that college go bankrupt, re-marry, while in his sixties have another kid, become a grandfather, be the host of the TV show, *Celebrity Apprentice*, get four hours of sleep each night (as he claims to do), appear as a guest on multiple TV shows, such as *Oprah* and *The David Letterman Show*, write a couple of books, run for president, **and** still find the time to track down and harass all of those women. Yeah, I don't think so, buddy. I mean, really? I can hardly plan out what I'm going to have for dinner, let alone go to a restaurant without asking someone I know how I like my burger cooked. Do you think someone with that busy a schedule is capable of finding time to do that?

If I could use one word for each party, I would describe the Democrats as being dependent and the Republicans as being dependable. The liberals are dependent on making sure that minorities feel like victims and that they are the only ones who can solve their problems. The conservatives are dependable and can see a problem before it can escalate and lead to a real thorn in the side. If I had to describe the two parties' judgment, I would tell you that the left has hindered sight, while the right has hindsight. The liberals are often unable to see the bigger picture and how they can affect the hardworking American. The Republicans, however, are prone to thinking, "how will this affect our citizens? How will this affect America in general?"

I know it sounds harsh, but it's all true. If you are a believer in the American dream, then you will know in your heart what I'm saying is true. The truth comes down to the basic principles of each American's right to "life, liberty, and the pursuit of happiness." Are *you* living your life? *Have* you the liberty to follow the American dream, *your* dream? And are *you* able to pursue whatever makes you happy without being afraid or ashamed to do so? If not, you are not being given your right, as a citizen of the greatest nation in the world, to the American dream.

# 2.

# THE ORIGINS

EVERY EVIL SUPER ORGANIZATION has its sinister origins. If you would like to know where the lies all started, look no further than the 1960s. The trend of fake empathy toward minorities can be traced back to when John F. Kennedy was running for president. When JFK was running for president in the 1960 election, a team of data scientists approached him with the vision of predicting what voters wanted to hear. Their data would allow for candidates to gauge which issues they addressed would appeal to more voting blocks. Doesn't that sound vaguely familiar?

On February 18, 1959, the Simulmatics Corporation opened.[1] Edward L. Greenfield, a thirty-one-year-old political consultant, had created the business with a vision that if you could collect enough data one day, the ability to predict anything might be possible.

Of course, Kennedy was a great president, but do you think he could have won the election on his own? The 1960 election results were the closest in history, with Kennedy winning the national popular vote by 112,827, a margin of 0.17 percent.[2] One of the talking points he was told was important was civil rights. Of course, you may be wondering why I accuse President Kennedy of false empathy. Well, I'm not. I am just saying that civil rights may not have been his initial priority. Clearly it wasn't, just look at his vice president!

You're most likely screaming into the pages of this book about how John F. Kennedy was an American hero, and any objection should be struck down with impunity. And usually, I would agree with you there. He made the ultimate sacrifice for the American people—a risk that every president knows they have when they take the oath of office. But it so happens that it doesn't end there.

The Kennedy family has remained a part of the political machine for years. It was only until US Representative John Kennedy III lost the race for the US Senate to Ed Markey would any member of the Kennedy family, for the first time, lose an election in the state of Massachusetts.[3] The tragic part of it is that the Kennedy line has only drifted further and further left.

I have considered JFK to be one of the few admirable and generally **honest** Democrats this nation has had. Right alongside FDR and, well…no one else. That's about it for me; FDR and JFK. Pretty sad, huh?

Meanwhile, across the political aisle, the Republican Party's history is strewn with ambitious men's names (so far) who made great strides that everyone is familiar with. Abraham Lincoln, the first Republican President and the Great Emancipator. Theodore Roosevelt founded *five* national parks—the most any President has ever established—because he was a "conservationist President."[4] Dwight E. Eisenhower understood the economic importance of interstate systems,[5] Ronald Reagan reunited a physically divided city by tearing down their wall,[6] George H. W. Bush made sure that the culprits of the worst terrorist attack this nation would pay, And Donald John Trump, who built back a depleted military, pulled our troops from countries we didn't need to be in, confronted China head-on, created the best economy the US has ever seen, united two nations that have been at severe odds for centuries, is securing our borders, and created 4 million jobs.[7] Now tell me, isn't that a list to be proud of?

To prove that I know there have been bad presidents on both sides, I'll name a few rotten Republicans. First, you have Nixon, who is still considered one of the most corrupt presidents in US history up to the time of this writing. Gerald Ford: What. A. Dummy. Need more be said about him? And George H. W. Bush, who wasn't extremely intelligent when his priorities concerned foreign affairs, was he? I hope that was a reasonable and decent list.

For those of you who haven't noticed yet, two of the heads on Mount Rushmore are Republican presidents. The other two are Independent and Democratic-Republican. Do you know why that is? That is because the Republican Party has done more for this country than any other party has. It seems that Republicans have been for everything the liberals say that we're against. We are anti-slavery, anti-segregation, pro-environment, pro-economy, pro-peace, pro-life, and pro-equal rights for all. Unfortunately for the Democrats, we aren't pro-stupid. We don't believe their lies. We aren't dummies.

If you would like to know where the origin of where social media hate comes from, I'll give you a little hint. It comes from individual people. I won't detail this topic in this section, but I will provide you with a few stories.

I consider myself to be politically informed. I have been told by even the most liberal of liberals that it's great that I fact-check. When I make an argument, I make sure I get my facts straight. I make sure I know what the hell I'm talking about before I slam someone for insulting my values. And when I don't know whether or not something someone says is true or made up, I'll just simply say that I haven't heard that and move on. How many Democrats do you think are willing or able to do that? When was the last time you can recall a Democrat admitting he or she was wrong? When was the last time you had one cornered in an argument on social media, and he or she didn't resort to throwing insults? It has been a while for me.

Take, for instance, what happened to me on social media once. On no particular day, I confronted someone on Facebook for claiming Antifa wasn't an organization and was just an idea. I told them, "I guess Antifa is a pretty harmful idea if people with a similar idea hurt so many Republicans." That response seems generally respectful, right? Anyways, that person responded by telling me I needed to "do an Independent fact check." One of their "friends" saw my comment and said my opinion was uninformed and illegitimate because I was young. Basically, because I was younger than they were, I cannot form my own opinions. That is hilarious coming from the party that thinks the minimum voting age should be sixteen, right?

Of course, that wasn't the only incident. I also was dragged into an argument over a post some loser had made, saying the pope was a pervert. I responded with, "So the leader of the Christian church, who has expressed his sorrow over the sexual abuse in the Catholic church, a man of peace, is a pervert?" The reaction I received was just plain near abusive: "Typical Christian to ignore the truth," along with, "Who the hell are you?!" and my personal favorite, the guy who insults your profile photo, "Who's this weird-ass kid? Who the *hell* thinks it's cool to wear a suit?" So I, one not so easily slapped around by an amateur, rolled back my sleeves for a single punch knockout, or so I had hoped. "Well, I'm sure that it's much more attractive when you take a selfie in front of your unflushed toilet." It was kind of stupid, I know. Unfortunately, that just escalated things further. I almost got to a point where I was going to tell them their opinions didn't matter. I dialed it down, fortunately, and apologized for even commenting on their stupid post. I ended up taking them off my Facebook feed entirely.

When I hear that Republicans are White supremacists, my blood boils. That is not true! Sure the KKK identifies as an alt-right group, but they didn't originate that way. The truth about how the Klan became alt-right is a little bit complicated to explain, so instead, I'll start with the origins of the Republican and Democrat Parties.

The Republican Party, as you may or may not know, was founded on March 20, 1864, in Ripon, Wisconsin, as an anti-slavery party. The Democratic Party was founded on January 8, 1828 by Andrew Jackson, who was, in fact, a slave owner. The Democratic party would continue to back slavery in the states until 1865, when the first Republican President, Abraham Lincoln, abolished slavery with the 13th Amendment. The parties would become divided within themselves when John F. Kennedy passed the Civil Rights Act almost one hundred years later in 1963. The Democrats in the party who had been pro-segregationists left and joined the opposite party. The Republicans that had been upset with the party for not doing that sooner joined the Democrats.

So essentially, the Republicans were stuck with the racist segregationists not by choice but by accident, and the Democrats received the Civil Rights activists. If you look at the official webpage for the Democratic Party, they describe their history merely. "For more than 200 years, our party has led the fight for civil rights, health care, Social Security, workers' rights, and women's rights. We are the party of Barack Obama, John F. Kennedy, FDR, and the countless everyday Americans who work each day to build a more perfect union. Take a look at some of our accomplishments, and you'll see why we're proud to be Democrats."[8]

If you noticed, they, of course, happened to omit the first one hundred years of their party. They start in 1920 with women's suffrage and go all the way to the *Affordable Care Act*. They clearly *haven't* forgotten about their party's racist past, and their refusal to ever talk about it is even more apparent. So what do they mean that they have led the fight for civil rights for the past 200 years? That's nuts! Only for the past sixty years have they cared about racial equality.

A party is not built on just its achievements but also the ability to admit to their discretions. Have they done that? No, they have not. The Republicans, however, on multiple occasions, are enthusiastic and willing to openly denounce White supremacists and any and all alt-right fascists in the party. They are an embarrassment to our party, and their votes in any election do not reflect the morals of the Republican Party, past *or* present. What these groups believe and say does not truly express the values of any American, I hope.

Now let me tell you my origin story. I was born on January 20, 2004, in the country of Russia. When I was thirteen months old, my biological mother left me at the neighbor's home and never came back for me. My mother was presumed dead, so I was put into an orphanage.

Let me describe a typical Russian orphanage to you. Most orphanages are overcrowded and undermanaged. There is very little color on the inside or outside of a building. At night, they put the orphans into a room crowded with other beds. The beds for the younger children have bars on them. Some are made of metal, and some are made of wood. You will never hear any crying in the orphanages in Russia. You never hear crying because the children, from a young age, learn that no one comes to comfort them. Some orphanages are better than others. Some are a bit more colorful than the rest. And this is all from my recollection.

One of the most tragic things about the Russian orphanage system is that 70 to 90 percent of the children in their system actually have biological parents who are still living.[9] The cheery name of the orphanage I was raised in was *Children's Home No. Four*. I stayed there until I was three-and-a-half years old, when, in 2007, an American couple adopted me. One of my earliest memories I have is of the first time I met them. Maybe I remember it because of the joy and excitement I had felt. Perhaps it was the sudden change from the feeling of being unloved that I had been accustomed to. Either way, it is one of my fondest memories.

In 2012, my father, or as I called him *Papa*, passed away from pancreatic cancer. This form of cancer is quick-acting if untreated or caught in its later stages. A year after he died, my mom and I looked for a clean start. We moved into a larger, new home in a better neighborhood. We adopted a dog and even got a pet bird. It seemed as if we had received the fresh start we had been after. I can not thank her enough for what she has done and continues to do in my life as my mom. If it weren't for her, I would still be in the system of the extremely socialist country, Russia.

Unfortunately for our family, it seems as if history has a way of repeating itself. In 2018, my grandfather was diagnosed with lung cancer that had originated from prostate cancer he previously had. He needed to get it immediately removed from his lymph nodes, which meant he would have to undergo surgery. At seventy-seven, my grandfather had never undergone surgery and was scared to have his first operation. He was categorically obese, had diabetes, and was in the twilight of his years. He was not what someone might describe as the perfect picture of health. He would admit that.

On the day of his operation, I admitted to myself that he had stood in as a father figure for me. The realization felt like a punch to the gut, to be honest. I had *always* looked up to my grandfather as a role model. But I had always thought that after my father had passed away, I would remain without a figure like that in my life. I understood I wouldn't have much time with him after that, so I vowed to tell him how I felt, one way or another.

After the surgery, it seemed as if they were able to remove cancer. I kept my promise to myself, and I soon thereafter told him what he meant to me. A few months later, at a routine checkup, a doctor found a spot in an x-ray, which he determined to be cancer. They decided they would go through a few standard tests to see if they could learn more. In Ohio, I was on a trip with my mom to meet her friends when we got a call from my grandparents. They had gotten the tests back. They told my grandpa he had a rare form of bone cancer that could not be stopped, only slowed down.

A few weeks before he died, I had a private conversation with him. During that conversation, he said, "I don't think God controls whether or not I die of cancer. I think these types of things are the results of decisions people make throughout their lives." He passed away on June 3, 2020, at 1:45 p.m. after a rapid decline in his health.

My grandpa helped me form my opinions. He helped me guide my way through politics. He is who I looked up to and who I wanted to be like. He was the perfect grandfather and ideal father figure for me. I will never fully understand the immense impact he had on my life, but just knowing that is a comfort. I would never care about what I do now if it weren't for my family.

My grandpa was a strong conservative, but he also was a strong man, no matter how physically weak he was. I never thought of him as dying, if you can understand that. A man or woman shouldn't be judged by their appearance but by the measure of their character. If you are caring toward others, you will always be strong, no matter how weak you become.

I know my grandpa encouraged me to do whatever I felt like I needed or wanted to do. Whether that meant to run his business one day or make my own legacy, he is just one of the many essential pieces of my life.

I don't mean to have a run-on like this and be sentimental in this chapter, *but* a crucial part of comprehension is understanding the past. How could anybody possibly understand the evolution of the Democratic Party and the Republican Party without a brief knowledge of the history behind them? And how might you understand and relate to what I'm saying and feel if you aren't able to dive into what made me who I am?

When people have the ability to describe how they have developed or why they believe what they do, they can explain their morals and values. That is what leads to open and productive discussions.

Before I die, I hope I can touch many people's lives the way my family members have touched my own. I hope that is what every person strives to achieve. But I'm sure a lot of people strive for power and recognition, groveling for praise, at the feet of the American people, begging for approval, unknowingly trained into submission by the hate they are exposed to every day.

# 3.

# In Case You Didn't Know

FOR YEARS NOW, THE Democrat elites have been peddling lies about their party, the Republican party, and our beautiful country. I have watched silently for years now the amount of hypocrisy the left feels that they are entitled to have. They have told us to be ashamed of America's past while they have never acknowledged their very own history.

Political figures, like Joe Biden, Elizabeth Warren, and Nancy Pelosi—just to name a few, have told you that White supremacists operate under the direct leadership of the Republican Party. Frankly, I'm disgusted with them, and you might see why. They act as if their agenda overrules the needs of others. They do not have a "plan" for how to solve every issue thrown at them, as they have told you they do. We, however, have adjusted with the times and continue to look out for Americans first. The Republican Party, as I have told you, was founded in 1854 as an anti-slavery movement, and the party's core values of upholding the Constitution and equal opportunity remain untouched.

While the White supremacists have moved away from the Democratic Party, they are not legitimate Republicans either. They only phased out from the Democrats because they, like the rest of us, have been fooled by the Democrats' flimsy *yet* effective disguise of the only party who mainly "cares about minorities." I have distant family members who have posted on social media that you are unequivocally and irredeemably a racist pig if you vote for the Republican Party.

The kind of thinking they engage is ultimately a tool of destructive and blunt force. It replaces any credibility that is present with contempt and suspicion. The very types of people who post this hostile rhetoric are only following their parties' top politicians' lead. The same leaders who should be setting an example tell you lies to gain control of *you*. Unfortunately for them, they have continued to insult you. We are tired of it, and it's time we finally express our frustrations.

Being ignored is not an option most of us are willing to take. We will be heard, and we will be understood. But unlike them, we will do it peacefully. We will do it through communication. Who we choose to lead us matters. Who we choose to be is the most essential tool of all.

Are you going to be destructive, chaotic, and useless? Or are you going to be constructive, firm, and productive? What you do is what people will think of your beliefs. Stand up and defend your party and beliefs. But do it the right way. Do it on the defense and not the offense. Because if you do, their lies will crumble. It will take a while, but they will.

To give you an example of the kind of lies the Democrats tell you, I've set up a list of a few people and their lies who are prime examples of what I mean.

**(Crazy) Nancy Pelosi**: This nut always created the false narrative that during the former president's administration, he was a liar and crook. She often mentioned invoking the $25_{th}$ Amendment because she thought he was "unfit." In fact, she once told the media that Trump was "morbidly obese." I might need to elaborate on this for you.

In mid-May 2020, President Donald Trump announced during a press briefing that he had begun taking a traditional anti-malarial drug known as hydroxychloroquine after consulting the White House physician. "I happen to be taking it...I'm taking it hydroxychloroquine—right now."[10] Hours later, in an interview with Anderson Cooper on *CNN*, Nancy Pelosi reacted to Trump's decision about taking the drug. "As far as the president is concerned, he's our president, and I would rather he not be taking something that has not been approved by the scientists, especially in his age group and in his, shall we say, weight group, morbidly obese, they say. So, I think it's not a good idea."[11] Give me a break, Nancy! First of all, since when did you care about his health? So stop acting like his mother! Second of all, I love just how polite you are; "in his, shall we say, weight group, morbidly obese."[12] That's rich! First, you take the high road by describing the condition of his body as a "weight group," then you drop the other shoe by body-shaming him, calling him morbidly obese, and third, I did an independent fact check on Trump's body mass index (BMI). Trump does not meet the definition of being morbidly obese. In fact, he just barely meets the definition of obese.

To be obese, you would have to have a BMI level of 30.0 or over. To be considered *morbidly* obese, you would have to have a BMI level of 40.0 or above. Considering Trump's age, height, and weight, his BMI level is only 30.1, a diagnosis of just obese, *not* morbidly obese, and not even mildly obese.

So, Nancy, I have a question. You have told us we need to listen to the science and doctors, right? Since when did you become a doctor? When did you get the right to decide what is and what isn't considered morbidly obese? You, Nancy, had just unwittingly fat-shamed any person who is slightly overweight. I guess you aren't as woke as you act, after all. I have to say to you is try focusing on doing your job–being a public servant–instead of worrying about how heavy someone is.

**(Sleepy) Joe Biden**: He claims he supports small businesses and blue-collar workers, and he would lower taxes. But if he gets his way, a small business owner who's selling their company could pay up to 50 percent in federal taxes.[13] One of his most blatant lies is when he tells you he supports our troops. According to *PolitiFact,* Joe Biden called a crowd of servicemen and women a "dull bunch," and told them to "clap for that, you stupid bastards" after bragging about his "great judgment."[14] Even if those comments were just "jokes," Joe, with his *great judgment*, should have known that's not appropriate. I know if I ever told that to even a single service member, I'd punch myself in the mouth.

One of Joe Biden's most ridiculous lies happens to be about his knowledge of his son, Hunter Biden's shady business deals with Ukrainian and Russian businesses. You would have to be in a coma not to know that during trips as the vice president to foreign countries, your son was spending his time using his connections to receive millions upon millions of dollars.[15] But I guess Joe had to have been asleep while this was all going on. Maybe Joe wasn't the most crooked vice president in history; perhaps he is just the most sleepy vice president in history.

**(Cheatin') Barack Obama**: One of Obama's biggest lies is just *now* being uncovered. It seems to appear that he *knew* Hillary Clinton and several Democrats were colluding with foreign intelligence officers. Obama knew this because former CIA Director John Brannon briefed him on Clinton's plan to concoct phony collusion. Recently declassified documents support these claims.[16] The truth about Barack—although hard to believe—is that he might just be the most corrupt president in the history of the United States of America, even more corrupt than Richard Nixon himself. This leads to speculation over whether or not he was aware that Hillary Clinton was using a private email server and knew what the emails related to.

**(Crooked) Hillary Clinton**: As a self-proclaimed feminist, Hillary Clinton made it her right to label any of her enemies as sexists and liars. And because of her self-proclamation, she personally sought to attack and discredit her husband's accusers. If she really is a feminist or a decent human being at all, then she should have been encouraging victims of sexual abuse to speak out instead of muzzling them.

Hillary Clinton's **big lie** is that she had deleted over 30,000 emails she claimed were personal. If I had to guess, I'd say that the emails were warning her about a possible attack that occurred in Libya on US soldiers back in 2012. These emails she decided were somehow less important than her campaign. She also claimed she deleted the emails before receiving a subpoena on March 4, 2015, ordering her to release all of her emails relating to the September 11, 2012 attack in Libya. She, in fact, had deleted her emails three weeks *after* receiving the subpoena.[17] If I had to choose a nickname for her, I wouldn't have called her Crooked Hillary. No, no, no. I would have preferred a catchier nickname, like "Straight to Spam Clinton" or "Down to Delete Hillary."

**(Lyin') James Comey** (this guy is a real tool): Disgraced former FBI Director James Comey knew about a note written by Bill Prietap regarding attempts to vilify Michael Flynn; yes, the very same note that ruined Flynn's career. The note reads as follows, "What's our goal? Truth/Admission or to get him to lie, so we can prosecute him or get him fired?"[18] That very note would have proven Flynn's innocence. Now all he had to do was disavow his loyalties, and Flynn's reputation wouldn't have been tarnished and dragged through the mud in a sham investigation. But truthfully, do they care? No, no, they don't.

**(Shifty) Adam Schiff**: Adam Schiff had, on multiple occasions, claimed that he knew of certain evidence that pointed directly toward mass Russian interference and collusion in the 2016 presidential election. Unfortunately for him and the fake news media that preaches this as the gospel truth, transcripts that were released by the House Committee of Intelligence prove otherwise. The transcripts basically show interviews taken during the investigations into the supposed collusion between Russia and the Trump campaign during the 2016 election contain material disproving the hoax.[19] So Adam Schiff knows there is absolutely no evidence of collusion, and yet he continues to spew his conspiracy theories everywhere. They call him Shifty Schiff for a reason.

With all of these examples, does anybody really think the Democrats are more honest than the Republicans? Who in their right mind wouldn't be concerned about this? You might not have known this because of the media. Of course, the majority of the media is run by liberals, who want nothing more than to have a Democrat-run country. The media tells way more lies than the people I told you about do. You'll read more about it in a later chapter.

These people have single-handedly torn apart the credibility of political offices. But of course, Nancy Pelosi would know about tearing things apart, right? I mean, who but Nancy Pelosi would tear the State of the Union before the American people? She's an attention hound! She literally has to be the center of attention wherever she goes. Any conversation about Trump, she throws in a shock just so she's talked about that night at the dinner table. She might just be, I think, psychologically unable to give a compliment to someone other than herself.

She is a lot like her cohort, Chuck Schumer. Let me tell you, Chuck is a lying clown who would be unappealing to the left if it wasn't for his constantly running commentary so polarizing it has its own magnetic force.

You might not have known that Donald J. Trump was one of the most straightforward presidents that this country ever had. In multiple interviews, years, and even decades before he ran for president, he was saying he would only run if the country really needed change. If someone had damaged the nation, he would run for president. At the final 2020 presidential debate, Trump said, "I ran because of you,"[20] referring to Obama and Biden. That is pretty honest, right? If you are having trouble deciding who is more personable, just look at the records.

# 4.

# "SHHH!" THE SILENT MAJORITY

THE EVENING OF NOVEMBER 8, 2016, a night I am sure you know well (it was downright unforgettable). It was the night the foundation of the Washington establishment began to crack. At the beginning of the election season, every liberal news channel prophesied Hillary's clean-cut path to win. She was up by six percentage points in the polls.

On election night, it was clear Trump would still win, no matter what the polls said. And it's not because of the electoral college. It's not because of any collusion hoax. It was because people didn't want a repeat of Bill Clinton. They didn't want a repeat of his lies. They didn't want someone who would screw them over as Bill Clinton had. It didn't matter that Hillary had been the secretary of state or was a "feminist." It didn't matter that she was a woman or an activist. What mattered was that she had stood up for one thing only in her life: her career and reputation.

The reason Trump won was that in swing-states, Democrats had come out in large numbers to turn on their heels and walk, *no*, run across the political aisle to stop Clinton. That's how Trump won the Electoral

College. The [few] Democrats who had voted for Trump had just become part of a growing number of people called the silent majority.

By its own name, the silent majority self-describes the people who are afraid to openly agree with what they know to be unabashedly true. According to Cato Institute surveys in 2017, 76 percent of strong conservatives and only 30 percent of strong liberals say the current political climate prevents them from saying things they believe because others might find it offensive. While an overwhelming 69 percent of strong liberals disagree with that statement, only 24 percent of strong conservatives disagree with that statement.[21] I personally find that to project a blatant suppression of freedom of speech.

In the current political climate, large crowds of radical far-left extremists are allowed to march in the streets, burn down communities, and attack or murder anyone who stands in their way. They go out of their way to find and destroy anyone with opposing views. They claim they do it because their voices go unheard and their cries for justice unanswered. Where is the justice for the lives and families they have decimated? Where are their supposedly "unheard cries"? I can tell you for a fact that the ones who are genuinely unheard are us: the silent majority.

The bias doesn't stop there, my friend. Liberals control institutes of teaching; that's indisputable. It's not just in colleges. It's not just in high schools either. It's in middle schools too, as well as elementary school. I know if you're reading this, elementary school seems like a stretch. But it's how teachers talk about what they're teaching. For example, if they educate children about what they see in our country, they add adverbs and adjectives. "This year has been full of *mostly* peaceful protests along with *very little* violent rioting." It's all about how they add "innocent" adverbs and adjectives to manipulate and form their students' opinions.

I've been a witness to this kind of liberal bias. Every kid has a teacher or teachers who don't like them. One school year was filled with teachers who weren't on my side. One teacher, in particular, who didn't exactly like me, was more than biased. Let's call her Ms. Oreo, shall we?

Ms. Oreo was the biology teacher. Toward the end of the school year, we were focusing on the ecosystem. I can't recall what we were being taught, but I do remember her announcing to the class about the next election cycle concerning global warming. "I won't tell you who to support, but I will tell you how to decide who you support. Remember that you don't always have to hold the same opinions that your parents or grandparents have..." she stated. "If your family doesn't believe that global warming is the most important issue, then you should probably consider changing your opinion." When she said that, I immediately inquired what she meant, and she replied with, "Somebody should not re-elect someone like our current president..." Yeah, sure, you did a great job not telling us who to support and not to support.

When Donald Trump became the president in 2016, the divide between the political parties had only grown. To be clear, it wasn't his fault. It seems as if Democrats were never going to give him a fair chance as president. Truth be told, we all know that it started before the 2016 election (I'll get to that in a later chapter).

I have watched as the nation has been torn apart between them and us, Trump and Biden, and Black Lives Matter and All Lives Matter, issue after issue, and day after day. And it shouldn't be this way. To begin with, the day Trump was inaugurated, riots broke out throughout the country. People were smashing up stores and setting objects in the middle of the street on fire. Plenty of so-called "activists" held signs, saying things, like, "No fascist USA!" and "Not my President!" Many Democrat politicians refused to attend his inauguration. Sure, Trump didn't participate in Biden's inauguration four years later, but neither man wanted the other to be there.

People wonder how this country got so divided. It's obvious. The Democrats have painted the Republicans as a power-grabbing, woman-hating, super-racist, xenophobic party of bigots, whose worst quality is that they have become mindless goons after having been brainwashed into being led by a womanizing fascist billionaire who was the most radical extremist conservative president in the history of the United States. Who can argue that it would be something to be legitimately divided over if that were the case? But that's not what conservatives did. I mean, seriously? It's not like we had elected Adolf Hitler to the highest office in the land. But the Democrats have created such a division that they can't even see from who the division came from. It's as if they're breathing in their own toxic gas and don't realize they're doing it.

The Democrats need people from the working class who'll listen to *all* political spectrum sides to lead their party. Then maybe they would be respectable again. They really need another Kennedy-type figure to be in their party. And I don't mean the current Kennedys either. There is an unbelievable number of Democrats who have been made so susceptible to the lies of the liberal media and their party leaders that they would vote for Joseph Stalin. They almost elected Bernie Sanders, so yeah, I guess they almost did elect a commie. But I suppose it's to be expected of never-Trumpers and Democrats to vote for someone who isn't Republican or Trump.

As I have found out in the great part of the past decade, the silent majority isn't just filled with quiet Republicans and turncoat Democrats. The silent majority is filled with a larger, diverse group of racial minorities than we initially thought.

According to annoying sitcom stereotypes and copycat television tropes, African Americans and Latinos are all alike and hate Republicans. They have portrayed a world where Black characters are in constant fear they will be attacked by law enforcement in a racial hate crime, where Latino characters hate Trump and are in constant fear of being deported, and where men constantly sexualize women. These familiar storylines depict racial and ethnic minorities as targets for discrimination and hate. They are made to look vulnerable and weak. I am just as tired of these stereotypes as I am of the constant attacks on my political convictions.

The fact is that it has become so hard to hide how the Democrats feel. Life-long Democrat minorities are rethinking their long-held political convictions. There is actually proof, despite what everybody has been led to believe. Unlike the Russian hoax, there is evidence of this. Thanks to national polling information, we have discovered that there has been a large amount of support gained for Trump and the Republican Party.

In 2016, only 10 percent of young Black voters supported Donald Trump. But unlike in 2016, during the 2020 election cycle, 21 percent of young Black voters supported Donald Trump. That's an increase of 11 percent—a large number if you think about it! In 2016, only 22 percent of young Hispanic voters supported Trump. But since then, that number has gone up by thirteen. Most recently, in 2020, 35 percent of young Hispanic voters supported then-President Trump.[22] You likely may not have heard those statistics yet because the liberal media has chosen to ignore them. That is just another reason to consider the Republican Party.

There is no doubt in my mind that the drastic increase in support is because of the 2020 election cycle. I'm sure a lot of young voters heard

Joe Biden loud and clear when he said, and I quote, "I tell you if you have a problem figuring out whether you're for me or Trump, then you ain't black."[23] Boy, oh boy, oh boy! How racist was that? Joe Biden, an old White man, just told the entire Black community that a): if you are Black and weren't going to vote for him, you are a race traitor, b): you don't care about racial equality and are anti-Black, or c): the entire Black community backs him.

That's as bad as the time he praised the Latino community for being more diverse than the Black community. "What you all know, but most people don't know, unlike the African American community, with notable exceptions, the Latino community is an incredibly diverse community with incredibly different attitudes about different things."[24] *Huh*? Has Joe been trying to incite a racial division between Hispanics and African-Americans? What I think Joe was trying to say is that Black people aren't uniquely diverse, and because of that, all vote the same way: *for him*. If they didn't, they must have some kind of weird genetic mutation that makes them think like a White supremacist but have a dark-skinned individual's outer appearance. Would I be accurate in my translation? That is something you should genuinely be concerned about.

I need to be honest with you. Kamala is in on it too. Yep. "But how can it be?" you ask. Well, to put it simply, it's her lack of empathy toward people that make her that way. In many ways, she's a Hillary Clinton 2.0, a second chance at a "woke" *female* president. And this time, she's perfect! Let's go down the checklist of qualities to make you the wokest candidate/VP nominee in the history of American election seasons.

- Are they a Democrat? *Check!*
- Are they liberal? *Check!*

- Are they a woman? *Check!*
- Are they the first woman to be in a particular position? *Check!*
- Do they happen to be part of a racial minority? *Check!*
- Are they the child of immigrant parents? *Check!*
- Are they anti-Trump? *Check!*
- Are they environmental activists? *Check!*

Holy cow! All she needs now is to be a member of the LGBTQ community, and she would be more woke than if Meghan Markle and RuPaul had offspring!

But thanks to a little thing called a record, Kamala quickly goes from being super woke to super ignorant. Before Senator Harris was a senator, she was actually a state attorney general for California. And before that, she was a district attorney. Before she was a D.A., she was just a prosecutor. Some say she was a "progressive prosecutor," some say she was just mediocre. But many people, including her, know she was actually a horrible prosecutor and an even worse district attorney.

Her record as a prosecutor shows she was overly aggressive when it came to prosecuting misdemeanors and felony convictions for marijuana possession, cultivation, and sale. It turns out her attorneys prosecuted and convicted 1,956 cases.[25] This record just confirms how uncompassionate she truly is. Aren't we supposed to help reform these kinds of behaviors, Kamala? Wait, I guess not. I mean, you yourself once "joked" about smoking pot, right? I guess only people who can't afford to go to rehab need prison time. To put it merely, Kamala Harris was never a "progressive" attorney. She only cared about creating an impressive record, whether it was right or wrong.

In a desperate attempt to make up for her old record of not giving a crap, she decided to start backing a fund posting bailing for BLM and

Antifa members who were arrested for violent offenses. Because of this, Timothy Wayne, a child rapist who was charged in 2015 for sexually abusing an eight-year-old girl, was released on bail.[26]

I hope I didn't trigger any woke liberals who are offended that I dared to criticize a woman of color who is the kid of two immigrants. But if I did offend anybody, remember, I didn't fault her for being a woman of color who happens to be the kid of two immigrants. I criticized her for being a bad person; that's true equality. She and I have vastly different backgrounds, but that doesn't mean I can't criticize her or her character.

Republicans aren't racist, we just don't believe that minorities should be treated like fragile snowflakes who can't pull their own weight in society because of "oppression." We believe that real oppression in America comes from treating minorities as groups of people who need a crutch to lean on.

Whatever ethnicity, orientation, race, or background a US citizen comes from, they are still Americans. Americans don't need a crutch to hold them up, they are able to stand on their own. That's how this nation was formed.

America was formed because like-minded people with determination and a vision of a more perfect union were able to support themselves. Remember, at one time, Americans were the minority in the eyes of the British. So, yes, I believe anybody and everybody who is a citizen of this country can damn well stand on their own two feet without being put into a protective bubble.

I don't give a crap if your feelings are hurt because I tell someone to pull their weight. If I can do it, so can anybody else. If another person can do something, then I sure as hell have the ability to do it. And it's not just those who have unique qualifications; it's all people who have the ability to pull their own weight.

A considerable part of the silent majority is made of the average everyday person, not anarchists or anti-government activists who are secretly plotting to overthrow our democracy. The silent majority is made of people who are scared to voice their opinions. People who are "politically correct" are the ones who interrupt you to tell you that you said something wrong. It has grown so out of proportion that I have to ask if I can still say something. For instance, recently, I found out that the term "master bedroom" is a racist term. It's more polite if you just say "owner's suite." I mean, who would want to speak their mind out if someone corrected you over something so stupid and insignificant.

These idiots are the same losers who protest just because some college professor used the words "sexual preference" instead of "sexual orientation." The very people who say being politically incorrect is harmful and suppresses minorities are the same people who would demand that you be fired from your job just for saying "Mexican" instead of "Hispanic." They are wildly afraid of free speech.

Two terms I made up that I think should be added to the universal dictionary and the list of phobias are *Oratoratychiphobia* and *Reipublicaeatychiphobia*. The first phobia I propose is Oratoratychiphobia: the fear of politicians being politically incorrect. The second, Reipublicaeatychiphobia, is the fear of *being* politically incorrect. As far as I know, there are no official phobias like this. Don't try to pronounce either word, for your sake. You could hurt yourself if you try. Just please don't ask me how to pronounce them either. I may have created the terms, but I didn't bother mastering the pronunciation of them.

Maybe a better way to describe snowflake liberals is "sensitive rioters." In all fairness to them, they genuinely are sensitive. They would burn down a building, but if you call them a rioter, they'll correct you and say they are moral superiors coming to receive reparations for past discretions.

More often than not, people, like Racheal Maddow, Keith Olbermann, Gretchen Whitmer, Nancy Pelosi, AOC, Mazie Hirono, J. B. Pritzker, and *CNN's* own Humpty Dumpty, Brian Selter, just to name a few, scream about political correctness to appear superior to others. For most people, that would be a huge turn-off.

# 5.

# WE DON'T BITE

THIS IS A SHORT CHAPTER, so when I say we don't bite, I'm not exaggerating. If you're a concerned citizen who just so happens to be a Democrat looking for another party, you're in luck. There so happens to be another party in the United States that's all-inclusive. In this party, you aren't rewarded simply for being a minority, but rather for your hard work. If you are looking for a change from empty, meaningless merits based on how oppressed you are, this is your party. The party I'm talking about is the Republican Party.

The Republican Party goes by several names. The most common terms are Republican, conservative, the Grand Old Party (GOP), and the right wing. If you are part of the Democratic Party, some names you might know us by are Nazis, fascists, bigots, racists, sexists, and some other terms I'm probably not allowed to list on this page. But have no fear; we are none of those things.

Just because we don't like to give an illegal immigrant a higher salary than a legal citizen, it doesn't mean we're racist. While we don't see the practicality of sanctuary cities, it doesn't necessarily imply xenophobia. And just because we generally hold every person, whether they're a man or a woman (or any of the other genders there are nowadays), to the same standard of work, doesn't mean we are sexists. Although we do support the freedom to practice any religion and defend all ethnicities, genders, and sexual preferences/orientations, I hope that doesn't mean we are bigots, Nazis, or fascists.

Being a Republican means you are a contributing member of society. You work to lower taxes (which is actually a good thing), push for equal income for everyone, and work not only for money but for the feeling of well-earned success. Some benefits you will receive are the perks of capitalism, a quiet life (if you want), and a slice of the American dream pie (without others taking from it). If you are worried about the big bad scary machine called capitalism, don't be. Capitalism is just another fancy word for you get as much as you work for.

Being a Republican means you don't have to be an activist to care about issues. When you are a Republican, you don't need to be "woke" or "triggered" by every little thing someone says just to be heard; we'll listen to you no matter what. No one in our party plans on calling you ignorant or just another cog of America's systematic racism. Nope, not us. But there is a flight risk in becoming a Republican. You will have to be part of serious conversations that don't adhere to political correctness guidelines. You will be called the worst names possible by the liberals.

Just to be clear, there are no accurate Republican stereotypes. We have members of the Black community, Latino community, immigrant community, LGBTQ community, and many more in our party. You just never hear about them because the left ignores them. And when they *are* acknowledged, they are called props by angry, raging liberals. Anyone is welcome to join the GOP. Sure, we are more traditional in our values, but just because some of us hold certain religious beliefs and some of us have certain convictions doesn't mean we won't allow you into our party.

I hope I made a convincing argument for those of you unsure whether or not the Republican Party is for you. If you have noticed, I try to be all-inclusive in my statement. But if you don't believe me *just* yet, maybe the rest of this book will help.

# 6.

# MARX MY WORDS,
# NOT JUST SOCIALISTS

KARL MARX ONCE SAID, "Accuse your enemy of what you are doing it, as you are doing it to create confusion."[27] Some things never change, do they? Karl Marx created the idea of Marxism in the nineteenth century. The fundamental foundation of socialism is that everyone gets paid the same amount as everyone else, no matter what job you have. So you can be a brain surgeon and not be paid fundamentally different than that of a preschool teacher. Socialism would mean everyone would get the same amount of healthcare, and I'm guessing the bare minimum. Socialism would create a world where people aren't allowed to make their own decisions, where hard work means nothing. Socialism has destroyed countries and ruined hundreds of millions of lives.

There were two very crucial periods in American history known as the Red Scare and the Cold War—I'm sure you've heard of both of them mentioned in your history class. During both of those periods, American citizens feared for their freedom. Communists infiltrated the government and caused panic. There seemed to be nothing that would stop the American-hating Marxists.

The only thing that stood in the way of the Communist takeover was both the Republicans and Democrats. Communism—which is ultimately based on socialist values—was not tolerated then. But for some reason, the ideology has begun to creep back into our beloved nation and has resumed its reign of terror all over again.

It has manifested itself into the appearance of activist groups, such as Black Lives Matter and Antifa. These are groups the liberal Democrats support on a national level. They say they want only equality, but they have taken more than just that. They have looted and burned down buildings and shops. They set police stations ablaze and have even taken over several blocks of the city in Seattle, Washington, calling it an "Autonomous Zone."[28]

These communists aren't activists. *Hell*, they aren't even progressive. They are dangerous extremists who want nothing more than to see America burn. For some reason, though, liberals don't get that. I guess if you use the Marxist/communist/socialist symbol on your organization's flag, it doesn't necessarily mean you subscribe to the ideology of that party; you know, the same ideology that is responsible for the ongoing genocide in China and the genocide that occurred in Russia under Stalin.

With that same logic, that would also mean a person wearing a white-hooded robe isn't necessarily a racist bigot but rather a civil rights activist. A skin head with a swastika tattooed forehead isn't an antisemitic a-hole, but rather a peace-loving rabi. Do you see where I'm going here?

Socialists hate our government, history, and even capitalism. They especially hate Republicans and the ideas of freedom. Socialism has become a growing anti-right movement that has sought to smother any opposition.

The socialists **hate** traditional Christian values. They feel that Christians are homophobic, anti-Semitic, sexist scum who want nothing more than to appease their God through the suppression of minorities. In fact, I think the Marxist socialists of today are merely Christaniphobic losers who are scared they'll be stuck with college debt for the rest of their lives.

Rather than hard work and perseverance, they'd instead take from those who have already put in the effort. Although stealing from the rich and giving to the poor sounds like something Robin Hood would do—it's not. It's something a communist government would do. The Marxists even admit that's what they want. Here's an anti-capitalist quote directly from the modern-day Marxist webpage, Marx21us.org, "We believe that workers create all the wealth under capitalism, which is a system run by a tiny, wealthy elite. A new society can only be constructed when we the workers collectively seize control of that wealth and plan production and distribution according to human need."[29] Do you *know* what that means?

They would start a revolution to overthrow our system of government. They would take what you earn and siphon it away. They would bottle feed any project or cause they feel needs to be front and center. You would work for the government and not for yourself. If they felt like it, they would seize your assets and take what you make. They would control every aspect of your life. That's how they would create equality.

To them, equality doesn't mean being given the same opportunities as everyone else; equality doesn't mean not being discriminated against. Equality to them means no one is allowed to earn more than anyone else. Nobody can be treated differently. That means if I don't feel a man should be allowed to walk into a girl's bathroom, I'm transphobic.

When Bernie Sanders lost the Democrat nomination, the socialists wept. But the most weeping came from Hollywood. Hollywood and California, in general, have become ground zero for socialist influences. For some inexplicable reason, entertainers, musicians, TV hosts, and movie stars have become socialist sympathizers. The amount of celebrities who have endorsed Bernie is unbelievable and just sad. These aren't second-class celebrities either; these are A-list celebrities. I have a list of some of the most well-known stars that had supported Bernie in 2020. Some may just shock and disappoint you; Cardi B, Hailey Bieber, Ariana Grande, Miley Cyrus, John Cusack, Danny DeVito, Dick Van Dyke, Kendrick Sampson, and Mark Ruffalo, just to name a few.[30] How sad is that?

Of course, celebrities would support socialism in its entirety. But they truthfully have no idea what they are supporting. They aren't middle-class workers. They don't have medium-wage routine jobs. They—and excuse my language—bitch and moan about how global warming is going to flood the entire West Coast and how children are locked up on the border. They brag about how they overcame all kinds of systematic discrimination to get where they are now. They praise Obama, their *lord* and *savior*, for being a shining beacon of hope for Black children all around the globe. They preach how they fight every day for the average underrepresented minority. They shame America for being a racist and irredeemable country of sin. But they know if they are ever forgotten, they'll have to resort to having lowly routine jobs like every middle-class American has.

To those celebrities who aren't crazy liberal activists and are Republicans, you are the ones who keep it real. And even those of you who *are* Democrats but still understand the responsibility you have, you are unique and authentic entertainers. But the people who abuse their platforms, you people stink.

These celebrities are some of the fakest people out there. But socialism has made its way into sports as well, mostly shown in professional football; yep, good ol' red-blooded American football. It comes in the form of anti-American protests from the athletes themselves.

When they kneel during the national anthem, they dishonor the men and women who gave their lives for our country. When they refuse to play games in protest, they get hailed as brave heroes who dare to stand up against systemic racism. They have single-handedly made a football game about protests.

Never mind the Americans who died in Afghanistan, they were anti-Muslim for fighting Islamic terror. Never mind the soldiers who fought fascism in WWII, they were anti-Semitic for not joining sooner. Never mind the rebels who fought the British for religious freedom, they were too Christian. Never mind the Union soldiers who fought to reunite the country and end slavery, they were systematically racist for not also fighting for civil rights.

Don't remember any of those people, just remember that police supposedly are systemically racists who hunt Black men and women just for a sadistic thrill. But seriously, people watch sports for pure entertainment and to be united in the fact that they want their team to kick the butts of the other team. They don't watch to protest or demonstrate. They watch to have a good time. They watch to escape the real world for a couple of hours. But when the athletes kneel during the national anthem, it ruins the whole point of sports.

All of these athletes, movie stars, celebrities, TV stars, and musicians are a load of hot hypocrisy. They use their influence to make political statements and sway opinions. The only thing they try and do is tell us how bad things are right now. I have a name for these kinds of celebrities; I call them hack-stars. They are hacks who act like they are the leaders of some type of social movement. But they aren't that; they're just wannabes who salivate at the idea to be on the news at night.

Joe Biden once said that "[Antifa] is an idea, not an organization." He made this comment, in full display of the American people, at the first 2020 Presidential Debate.[31] He allowed himself to give the middle finger to the American people and say, *screw you!* He fundamentally told the world that he doesn't care about the people who this group has hurt.

Not only is Antifa a socialist Marxist organization, but it is now a terrorist organization. Now, if anyone commits a heinous act of violence in the name of Antifa, they are tried as terrorists. While this was a move made by Trump I back wholly, others think it is proof that the former president is a fascist.

I have heard the argument that Antifa isn't an organization because it doesn't have a sign-up sheet. And I have listened to the argument that says it is. To those two arguments, I agree with the latter. I believe Antifa *is* an organization. An assortment of violent activists who believe that the only way for them to achieve their ideological goals is through violent and harmful means is totally organized and not at all random.

You don't need a sign-up sheet to be part of an organization in every case. Do you need a sign-up sheet to be part of the brotherhood of man? Do you need to sign up to be any particular religion? Could an Islamic terrorist bomb a school and then claim he was acting on behalf of the Christian faith? You don't need to register as a terrorist to be one. If someone who claims to be an Isis member doesn't "join" Isis before shooting up a nightclub, does that mean they aren't an Isis terrorist? If you subscribe to the beliefs of a group of similar-minded people, you are, in principle, one of them. Do neo-Nazis have a signup sheet? It's like if I said that being a Nazi is just an idea and not an organization. You don't need leadership to be an organization.

Just to convince you that Antifa is an organization, I did some research. Antifa has several roots throughout history, mostly in Germany. But first, I'll give a quick explanation of the beliefs of Antifa. They believe that fascists aren't privileged to the right of free speech and assembly because of their oppressive views that silence the rights of others. They believe that views and opinions actually hurt people! Views only hurt people if they encourage violence. They also believe the only way for change to occur is by forcibly making people change. Although they believe in equality, they push for the same kind of equality that is rooted in socialism.

The cult-like extremist movement known as Antifa has become relevant in the current political climate. The history behind this group is what created the monstrous radical anarchists that we all have come to know and love today. Antifa was first called *Antifaschistische Aktion,* German for "Anti-Fascist Action," in 1932 by the Stalinist Communist Party of Germany (known as the KPD back then).

Their sole purpose was originally to gain control over other political parties in the Weimar Republic they deemed as fascist. During this period, Hitler was the leader of the Nazi Party, so naturally, the Nazis controlled Germany. The original intended use of the Anti-Fascist Action was to challenge the Nazi Party and fascism. Instead of just combating Nazis, they began to challenge members of other political parties. They attacked conservatives, liberals, and just about anybody who refused to join them. Antifa, back then, was only short-lived and would quickly go into hibernation for several decades before resurfacing.

In the 1980s, after being reestablished from autonomism, Antifa would renew support in Germany. It was that generation of Antifa where the very same tactics they use today would come into practice. They began to hold protests, and riots formed in large groups, populated by rioters dressed in black.

Now around the same time during the '80s, there was a similar movement. It actually developed from the efforts of punks in the music industry to remove neo-Nazis and other White supremacists. In an attempt to do that, the Anti-Racist Action (ARA) was born. It didn't stay contained long in the Midwest before other branches formed as it spread throughout the country. Groups like the Midwest Anti-Fascist Network (MANF), which was founded in 1995, only helped to push their propaganda.

Created from whatever remained of terrorist organizations, such as Weather Underground, Black Liberation Army, and the FALN, the John Brown Anti-Klan Committee (JBAKC) was established. It was only when the JBAKC and The MCO (May 19th Communist Organization) became part of the AR would any real chaos ensue.

The MCO operated under the excuse that they were fighting for "black liberation." They were the perpetrators of numerous attacks in the '80s that included bombings and robberies. They were directly responsible for the 1981 Brinks armored car robbery. They would use what they had stolen to fund their radical extremist agenda.

The JBAKC had gone a little further than their counterpart, MCO. They had their own newsletter, "Death to the Klan!", which they used to spread propaganda. They would go on to accuse Reagan of White supremacy and encourage the MCO to continue their bank robberies. They would also publicly support communist uprisings in other countries, like Nicaragua and El Salvador. And while they claimed to be doing it to fight oppressive fascists and White supremacists, all they were really doing was creating anarchy and discord.

Fast forward to the mid to late 2010s, Antifa has still been allowed to run rampant. Their message today is that police officers are just Klansmen who wear badges. They run on the idea that the government is built on racism. And while Antifa is as strong as ever, it has only gotten there through an unexpected turn of events.

The ARA ended up dissolving any leadership they had, and through a leaderless movement, Antifa has built up a cult-like following. The lack of any obvious leadership has made Antifa seem less sinister to the left, which has been blind to all kinds of communistic movements for decades now.[32]

The left has become so dismissive of Antifa that even Portland might have an Antifa mayor! Yeah, scary. Sarah Iannarone, who is at this time, a candidate for the position of the mayor of Portland City, is running against the current Mayor Ted Wheeler. She also happens to be part of Antifa.

In a city torn apart by rioters and anarchists, you'd think a person like that would be run out of town on a rail, right? Well, apparently, that doesn't matter. Destruction and havoc don't matter to the man who allowed these riots to happen, Ted Wheeler, and apparently, it doesn't matter to Sarah Iannarone, who dismisses the violent riots as "peaceful protests."

In her own words, here is how she explained why she's an Antifa member. "To those who say Antifa are violent thugs: I am not a violent thug and I am Antifa. I am Antifa because the Red Hats are coming after brown & black people, after Jews, after queer & trans people, and more. They are coming after our democracy. #HolocaustMemorialDay, #NeverForget."[33] Might I just say thank you, Sarah Iannarone? Thank you for everything. Thank you for confirming what we have known all along: your party runs on hate and the manipulation of minorities and public opinion. "The Red hats are coming"? Are you talking about us, Republicans? Or did you just misquote Paul Revere?

The last time I checked, hunting down Black, brown, queer, and trans people wasn't on the Republican agenda. In fact, I don't think the Republican Party has ever had room on their checklist for "come after minorities." You know, what with all the contributions to the Black community and immigration reform that we have worked hard for, I really don't think we've had the time to do any of those things. Unless I missed the part in my history book where it says, Abraham Lincoln was actually a Democrat and Republicans were pro-slavery, shut up, Sarah!

Sarah Iannarone, like many blind, dumb, and deaf Democrats, likes to say that Antifa isn't made up of violent thugs. Well, please tell that to the hundreds of Republicans that have been hurt, attacked, and intimidated by this terrorist organization. Domestic terrorism is in the United States, and it's in the form of neo-Nazis, Antifa, the Ku Klux Klan, and BLM. Some are more dangerous than others. For instance, BLM is made up more of anarchists than domestic terrorists.

Black Lives Matter (BLM), was founded on July 13, 2013, by Alicia Garza, Patrisse Cullors, and Opal Tometi.[34] BLM is a so-called left-wing "activist" group that supposedly advocates social and racial reforms through "peaceful" protest. Well, from what I can see, Black Lives Matter is just another extremist far-left organization and another way for socialist Marxists to get their way.

When I tell you I don't like Black Lives Matter, I don't mean I hate Black people. To me, *all* lives matter. That means Black lives matter, White lives matter, Asian lives matter, Latino lives matter, Christian lives matter, Jewish lives matter, Muslim lives matter, Buddhist lives matter, Atheist lives matter, trans/gay/lesbian/bisexual and queer lives matter, police lives matter, fire fighter lives matter, the president's life matters—whoever it is—unborn lives matter, male lives matter, female lives matter, Democrat lives matter, Republican lives matter, liberal lives matter, conservative lives matter, your life matters, and my life matters. When I say I dislike BLM, I mean I hate what they have done, I hate their tactics, and I hate the destruction they have caused. What they demand—BLM is just one of the many causes for buildings being set on fire, for weeks of endless riots breaking out, and a contributor to the massive division in this country.

On May 25, 2020, a Minneapolis police officer kneeled on the neck of a local forty-six-year-old Black man. George Floyd died after eight minutes of the police officer kneeling on his neck. When the footage of this abhorrent miscarriage of justice came out, the entire nation was in shock, not just Democrats but also Republicans.

I was shocked. I was horrified by the abuse of power and cruelty this officer had shown. To give you an idea of how long eight minutes is, that's about the length of two average commercial breaks. I felt extremely saddened by what I had seen. I had expected there to be protests, and why shouldn't there be? But what came next came nothing close to what I expected. Riots broke out. Looters broke into stores, department, grocery, and mom and pop shops. I thought the chaos would stay contained in Minnesota, but hell was I wrong. Within days, cities across the country experienced the kind of mayhem the city of Minneapolis was faced with.

As I watched my city of Chicago being overrun by looters, agitators, and rioters, I felt an overwhelming sense of uncontrollable rage. It would've been one thing if the police could've controlled it—but they couldn't. I watched as squad cars sped past stores being looted.

There was so much crime that the police had to actually stand back and watch it all go to hell. It seemed as if nobody was doing a thing to prevent the violence. Mayor Lightfoot did have the Guard called in but she refused to let them do their job. "They will not be actively involved in policing and patrolling." Then why did you call them in?! And our idiot Governor—J. B. Pritzker—was quick to blame Trump for the riots. Let me tell you a little something about our governor. In Illinois, there are eleven billionaires, six of whom are Pritzkers. Out of those six Pritzkers, J. B. is, without a doubt, the dumbest. He is an unintelligent, clueless, moronic twit who hasn't the brains to run an entire state, let alone one city. He doesn't know what he's doing, and he never has a plan. I'm sure he doesn't even know the difference between his head to his backside. For being a Democrat in Illinois, plenty of Democrats dislike him. The day after the first horrible night of the riots, Pritzker issued a statement urging anybody involved in the riot to get a Covid-19 test and quarantine.[35] He didn't say to cease and desist. He didn't say it was destroying the city. No, he was worried that the rioters might get sick—what a joke.

BLM has been responsible for the death and injury of many innocent people. They don't care who they hurt. They don't care if what they do affects a White or Black family. Let me tell you a story about one person killed during a BLM riot. Here is an excerpt from Ann Dorn, the wife of Police Officer David Dorn, who spoke at the 2020 Republican National Convention:

Hello, My name is Ann Dorn. I'd like to introduce you to my husband David. Father of five. Brother to 12. Grandfather of 10. Friend to thousands. He was the most kind, dedicated, loving life partner I could ever hope for. He had a big smile and a heart to match. He was blessed with the gift of gab, and that gift enabled him to touch souls and inspire people, especially young people. Oh, how he loved kids. And they loved him back.

Dave was all about service. He served thirty-eight years in the St. Louis Metropolitan Police Department and six years as Chief of Police at the Moline Acres Police Department. After forty-four years, he retired from law enforcement, but he never retired from helping a friend in need.

Since he befriended every person he met, he was a very busy man. One example of that was his friendship with a young man named Lee. Dave met him when Lee was just a kid, after members of his family were attacked and murdered. Dave took a special interest in the boy. They bonded, and their friendship grew and remained strong through the years. Lee eventually opened a pawn shop. He trusted Dave implicitly and asked him to help with security. Dave readily agreed.

Whenever the shop's alarm would go off, the alarm company called Dave, and he would investigate. If he got a call after I went to bed, he would wake me up to tell me he was going to Lee's shop to make sure everything was alright. Most of the time, they were false alarms—triggered by storms or animals—but I never rested easy until I heard Dave's key turn to unlock the door.

The alarm that went off the morning of June second was for real. It was a violent night in St. Louis. four police officers were shot. Others were hit with rocks and fireworks. At least fifty-five businesses were damaged, looted, or set on fire. As the Officer of Wellness and CIT Coordinator with the police department, I was keenly aware of the rioting and spent the evening getting ready to mobilize support efforts for officers who were impacted. After I had gone to bed, Dave received a call from Lee's alarm company. The front door of the pawnshop had been breached. This time, he didn't wake me up to tell me. He probably knew I would have tried to stop him or insisted on going with him.

As I slept, looters were ransacking the shop. They shot and killed Dave in cold blood and live streamed the execution and his last moments on this earth. Dave's grandson was watching the video on Facebook in real time, not realizing he was watching his own grandfather dying on the sidewalk.

I learned of all this around four a.m. when our doorbell rang. The Chief of Police was standing outside. I wondered why Dave had not answered the door. It wasn't uncommon for him to be up watching TV at that time. I called out to him several times. No reply. He wasn't there. I let in the Chief. Fighting back tears, he uttered the words every officer's spouse dreads.

I relive that horror in my mind every single day. My hope is that having you re-live it with me now will help shake this country from the nightmare we are witnessing in our cities and bring about positive, peaceful change.[36]

Oh, and by the way, Officer Dorn was an outstanding *American* citizen. He may have been Black, but that didn't matter to the murderers, the murderers being Black and BLM "activists." They sadistically live-streamed his execution. That is something a terrorist would do. But what are they? To the protesters, they are heroes for standing up against the system and fighting systemic racism. They feel as if their actions have no real-life consequences. They took away the brother of twelve, father of five, and grandfather of ten.

Imagine that for a second. When my grandpa died, I was beside myself. Imagine that feeling only ten times worse with the added surprise and burning rage that comes from a lack of justice. That's how the ten grandchildren probably felt. That's probably how his brothers and sisters felt. And that's probably how his spouse felt.

BLM is just another tactic to divide America, plain and simple. I would be a supporter if it actually just supported what they said they do. But they don't. When you demand things like defunding and abolishing the police, you're off your rocker. When you burn down a police precinct and take over several city blocks, you're an extremist.

The fact that BLM was able to take over an entire portion of the city of Seattle and force people who lived there to pay for protection is nuts! What's worse is the mayor called it the "Summer of love"![37] My God, how radical have these liberal mayors become?! So I ask you this: Is BLM a movement for change or a movement to push for an overthrow of government?

When I tell you socialism is bad, I mean it's bad. It is one of the worst things that could happen to our country. It's a truly scary thought that socialism is becoming a part of our government. Everywhere you look in the Democrat Party, one way or another, socialism is there, whether it's in dealing with social justice or the economy.

It's in our schools, the news, and our universities. It's there because of people, like Joe Biden, who has corrupted everything he has touched during his forty-seven year in Washington, or Bernie Sanders, who pushes for socialized medicine and free college for all. If you only take one thing from this book, let it be how dangerous socialism is.

Socialism is the deterioration of individual independence, destruction of incentive, and abolition of everything this country is founded on. The freedoms of life, liberty, and the pursuit of happiness would be nonexistent in a socialist America. The right to speak your mind out would be closely monitored by the left. Our country didn't declare independence, fight a civil war, join two world wars, attack terrorism, and abolish slavery just to become a communist country.

If you believe the American dream is still alive, you will reject the left and their socialist agenda. If you still have faith in your government, you will fight for your right to hold an opinion. If you believe in equality, you will stand next to those who are treated less than others. If you believe in truth and justice, you will look for it and not just accept what you hear as the truth.

If and when patriotic Americans, like you, stand up to them, our country will never become a socialist country. You are the government, you choose who leads it, and you get to decide what path our country goes down. You stand between the annihilation of our democracy and the prosperity of our nation. No one but you has that power.

# 7.

# F̶A̶C̶T̶U̶A̶L̶ FAKE NEWS

ZEUS HAD HIS LIGHTNING, the cavalry has their swords, North Korea has its nuclear missiles, and the left has the media. What do these all have in common? They are all weapons of destruction. To them, the media is not a tool that can be used for the good of humanity. The media is another way to spread their propaganda, clear and simple. Media includes social media, news media, and entertainment media. That's a wide variety of bases to cover. And since they don't report on it, why don't I?

To the left, the news media is the ultimate weapon of destruction, chaos, and panic. The news media's muse is the far-left's lies. They constantly push the disinformation, lies, and fear to control the masses. While they are doing that, they throw in a few of their own, just for the heck of it. While they vary on what they claim is the truth, they are clear on one thing: A Democrat *never* lies (except Cuomo). It's funny, when confronted about their obvious bias, they're quick to cover their asses. I wish they'd be just as fast to cover their mouths before lying to us.

The motto they should have is, "see no evil, hear no evil, speak no evil." They clearly refuse to see any wrongdoing on their behalf.

They would have to be deaf to not hear the baseless crap they are pushing. And they do everything they can to avoid reporting any crap the Democratic Party is responsible for. They hide the truth from the American people, and it's getting worse every day.

When I say they never report any wrongdoing, I don't expect them to cover their bias on TV. No one expects them to do that. I do, however, expect them to report the facts, not just the facts they like, but the facts that people need to be aware of. That even goes for Republicans as well. Report on the news, not your opinions.

It cannot be overstated enough that there is a clear and present bias in the world of news media. In a report by *Knight Foundation*, 44 percent of the media seen on TV, in newspapers, and on the radio is perceived to be inaccurate by Americans. Sixty-four percent of the news presented on social media is thought to be biased.[38] If 44 percent of news outlets are thought to be biased, then who do we believe? I, for one, think it's a good idea to get both sides of reporting.

I'm embarrassed to say that I listen to liberal media as well as conservative media. I know, I know, it's a sin to do such a horrible thing. Besides that being a taboo, it must seem pretty confusing to do such a thing. But I find that it gives me an idea of what is and isn't reported, although I do hear more facts reported on *Fox News* than any liberal news source would ever.

One of the worst things I see on TV today is the liberal talk shows. Shows like *Saturday Night Live*, *Jimmy Kimmel Live!*, *The Tonight Show Starring Jimmy Fallon*, *Good Morning America*, *Late Night with Seth Myers*, *The Late Show with Stephen Colbert*, *The Daily Show with Trevor Noah*, *Full Frontal with Samantha Bee*, *Real Time with Bill Maher*, and a whole load of others constantly berate the office of the president, and more often than not, anyone who's opinion they disagree with. They lampoon Trump and compare his supporters to the equivalent of Nazis and White supremacists.

I was turned off by *SNL* (sad not laughable)—which evidently has a debilitating bias—*years* ago. The show's writers (if you want to call them that) literally cannot go a single episode without mentioning Donald Trump. They have lost their souls. They have lost their comedy. They have lost their humor. And because they have lost that, they have also lost their comedic appeal to many Americans. They do not give a fair voice to both sides. They often refuse to poke fun at the Democratic Party. These shows are chock-full of hack stars. They honestly have become an extension of the arm of the Democrat Party. They don't even try to hide their bias. Jimmy Kimmel, nightly, has a joke about Trump.

There was one point during the pandemic when Jimmy Kimmel was hosting *Jimmy Kimmel Live!* from his own home, and was out to "spend more time with his family." Yeah, sure. How much time with your family are you truly missing out on? You're telling us you aren't with your family enough even though we're in the middle of a pandemic, and you even host your show at home?

While he was gone, he had guest hosts who would run things for him a couple of nights a week. While most of the guest hosts were Jimmy-clones who imitated Kimmel's usual material, there was one, in particular, that wasn't like the rest. Sebastian Maniscalco was a breath of fresh air. I was blown away by how original he was. He was funny, politically incorrect, respectful, and most of all, *not* political. Not a lick of politics came out of his mouth. I was hoping he would permanently replace Kimmel. Hey, a guy can dream, right?

A recent study taken by the Center for Media and Public Affairs at George Mason University on the expanse of jokes targeting Trump shows an outrageous amount of bias among these late-night stars.

Between Stephen Colbert and Jimmy Kimmel in 2016, about 77 percent of marks were made about Trump, and only 22 percent were related to Hillary Clinton.[39] Now I know what you're thinking, "That's **unbelievable**. And nobody does anything about it?" Well, no, they don't do anything about it. In fact, they have done the exact opposite of doing something about it.

The greater part of 2020 was spent mocking a single man. In one month alone, a whopping 455 jokes were about Trump. To no ones' surprise, only a disappointing fourteen quips were about Joe Biden. To add on to that, sixty-four more jokes were made about the then-president's family. So 97 percent of the jokes were directed toward Trump, only 3 percent were about Joe Biden, **and** that was just in the month of September![40]

Now I can imagine your shock; I was shocked too. How could so many jokes be told about Joe Biden? Don't they know that he's going to bring America together? Well, to that, I say the only reason America needs to be reunified together now is because they tore it apart! They wonder why Trump attacked them on Twitter. He attacks them because, before even the election, they were attacking him and his family.

I used to watch Jimmy Kimmel, but now I can't even stand the mention of his name without cringing. I can't stand him because all he does is rant and complain. He reprimanded the former president for supposedly "encouraging" violence, and yet he himself refused to reprimand the rioters and looters for tearing apart cities. I, for one, think Jimmy is a no-talent, Johnny Carson wannabe. But he is never going to be anything like Carson.

Unlike Kimmel, Carson held himself to the high yet simple standard of keeping politics out of the show. And that goes for Stephen Colbert, Jimmy Fallon, and the rest of them as well. Try a topic other than politics for once, and perchance you people would get higher television ratings if you did. Then again, maybe they just aren't that funny.

Social media is the universal bulletin board of community sharing. Want to post a picture of your cat stuck inside an empty Kleenex box? Social media is for you. Are you looking for a place to post your family vacation photos for the whole world to see? Social media is definitely for you! Are you looking for a place to share your conservative views? Then social media is not the place to go. Only if you have liberal thoughts can you be given the right to free speech. I know that it seems unfair, but those are the rules. I didn't make them. No, the people who made those rules are Mike Zuckerberg of Facebook, Jack Dorsey of Twitter, and Google of YouTube.

The power they wield is so immense they need to be considered monopolies. The three of them are like the Holy Trinity of social media: the Father, the Lord Almighty himself, Jack Dorsey, the Savior, Mike Zuckerberg, and the Holy Spirit, which is a part of us all, YouTube. They are, in point of fact, more like the three heads of Cerberus, the tri-headed dog who guards the entrance of Hell in Greek mythology.

YouTube, Twitter, and Facebook have taken a liking to the idea of an authoritarian rule over their users. If someone they don't like posts something they also don't like, they figure others won't like it either, so they take it down. If someone they **really** don't like posts something, anything really, they might lock them out of their account, just for kicks.

Twitter has a record of blocking conservative users on their platform. They even became used to locking and blocking the **president of the United States**. Twitter has no shame. Trump was blocked dozens of times in the four years of his presidency. Below is a list of articles that report on specific posts that have been blocked or flagged on Twitter from prominent conservatives.

- Twitter locks official Trump campaign account over sharing Hunter Biden video[41];
- Twitter censors Trump's tweet knocking Supreme Court's Pennsylvania vote. Facebook also cracks down[42];
- Twitter, Facebook have censored Trump sixty-five times compared to zero for Biden, study says[43];
- Twitter briefly suspends CBP Commissioner Mark Morgan after he touts success of border wall[44];
- Twitter censors Trump's Minneapolis tweet for "glorifying violence"[45];
- Trump campaign press secretary temporarily suspended on Twitter over mail-in voting tweet[46];
- Twitter locks out Kayleigh McEnany from her personal account for sharing New York Post's Hunter Biden report[47];
- Twitter exec in charge of effort to fact-check Trump has history of anti-Trump posts, called McConnell a "bag of farts"[48];
- Twitter dings Trump tweet on voting in North Carolina: "Voting twice in North Carolina is illegal"[49];
- Twitter locks out McConnell's campaign for posting video of calls for violence at his home[50];
- Twitter deletes video promoted by Trump on hydroxychloroquine use for coronavirus[51]; and
- Twitter slammed for "shadow banning" prominent Republicans.[52]

That's a lot of articles relating to Twitter's abuse of power. You might wonder why I used almost an entire page to show you this. First of all, I did it to give you an idea of how widespread the bias is. Second of all, it's a great filler for the book. It tells the story of a social media tyrant bent to silence political opposition. It shows the constant attacks that Republicans are under. It offers a look into the massive amount of indifference to the office of the president of the United States there is among big tech giants.

The elitists who run big tech corporations look down their noses at us ordinary citizens and sneer. They think they are superior, but if you stand back, they are all snobby stuck-up losers who believe that we won't notice them messing with our lives. We see what they indeed are; we know the truth. Because of that, we won't allow them to silence us anymore.

We are at a crucial point in history where we are at the end of our rope with the tech-monopolies controlling the flow of information; information that is constitutionally our right to know. We have a right to know the type of things are going on. Hiding behind the Democrat Party won't protect them any longer. Acting like the government is not their job. After the years of the suppression they have put us through, they finally are being held accountable.

On Tuesday, November 17, 2020, Jack Dorsey and Mark Zuckerberg testified in front of the Senate to explain their roles in trying to sway the election and voters. Even after the election, Facebook still made efforts to silence Conservative voices who felt as if the election was stolen from their candidate. Groups like "Stop the Steal" and others were suppressed in ways that made it harder for a person to locate them, so unless they were genuinely looking for them, they wouldn't be able to find them.[53] So is social media a good or bad thing? It has the potential to be both.

Recently, findings that directly linked Joe Biden to his son's business dealings in China, Ukraine, and Russia, were released—two findings in fact. One of them was about emails found on Hunter Biden's laptop, which you might now know as the laptop from hell. The other was about Tony Bobulinski, a former partner of Hunter Biden.

Both stories were initially featured in the *New York Post*. When they tried to post it on Twitter, they were locked out of their account. That meant that they weren't allowed to "tweet" at all until they deleted posts related to their article. Furthermore, they blocked the article from even being posted on their platform. They censored free speech on their platform, and in doing so, became an oppressive force.

The *New York Post* was blocked from posting on Twitter for sixteen days before they were set free. When Twitter explained why they locked the *Post* out of their account, they said they had violated their "hacked material" policy.[54] *Bullsh\*t!* They don't follow their policy very well then.

When the *New York Times* released Donald Trump's "taxes," Twitter never blocked those articles. If the released taxes were real, the only way they could have possibly been obtained was illegally. So what is it? Did they illegally obtain the tax returns? Or did they make them up? I'd say they were just made up to support another phony leftist narrative, like the Russian collusion hoax. Why didn't Twitter block posts related to that? Because they are incredibly biased!

To put it simply, when was the last time you heard of a high-profile Democrat being blocked? Why hasn't Congresswoman Alexandria Ocasio-Cortez had any of her posts blocked? What about Ilhan Omar? Kathy Griffin never faced repercussions on social media for her now-infamous photo of her holding a decapitated dummy head that resembled President Donald Trump. Was she ever blocked or locked out of any of her social media accounts for the multiple death threats she made against the president of the United States? No, she wasn't. The most they did was flag her posts as "potentially sensitive." I am, however, glad to say that she was blacklisted in Hollywood for her abhorrent behavior. She was fired from *CNN* and put on the no-fly list as a potential terrorist.

While everyone else did the proper thing, Twitter was the one to show their bias right out in the open. I would never—no matter how much I dislike someone—wish harm upon them; most reasonable people would agree. But that seems to be it for Hollywood.

Not one Democrat lifted a finger to confront Johnny Depp when he implied he was thinking about assassinating the president. "When was the last time an actor assassinated a president? Now I want to clarify, I am not an actor. I lie for a living. However, it's been a while, and maybe it's time."[55] Did Madonna receive any liberal backlash after acknowledging the idea of blowing up the White House?[56] No, she did not.

It seems as if all of Hollywood has forgotten that threatening the United States president is a federal offense. But if these hacks were actually held accountable for their messages of killing the president, Hollywood would be empty. So why doesn't Twitter or Google hold these people accountable? They wouldn't lose any ground if they did. Unless they want hatred, bias, and intolerance to spread, they should take a good look at these public figures.

I would love to tell you that this sort of bias is rare. I really would. Because if it was rare, I wouldn't have had to write a chapter on it. But it's a real issue, despite what "research" might show. The biggest evidence of bias is that these social media giants had the audacity to block the (former) **president of the United States**. They have, over time, blocked the White House press secretary, Donald Trump Jr, *Fox News*, Laura Ingraham, the *New York Post*, loads of other conservative politicians, and much, much more. But that doesn't seem to matter to them. What seems to matter to them is not their blatant suppression of information but rather Russians setting up fake accounts.

I once found an example of liberal bias on the search engine *Google* by accident. I was about to start research on Alexandria Ocasio-Cortez, so I began to search "why aoc is..." but before I could finish, I noticed the suggested searches—you know, the ones Google gives. They gave practically glowing reviews. In this order, the suggestions were, (1) why aoc is a good leader, (2) why aoc is inspiring, (3) why aoc is a great leader, (4) why aoc is a good role model, (5) why aoc is important, (6) why aoc is important, (7) why aoc isn't a good leader, and (8) why aoc isn't a socialist.

When I saw that I paused for a moment. I opened a *Yahoo!* search engine and typed in the same thing, "why aoc is." The suggestions confirmed my suspicions.: (1) why aoc is crazy, (2) why aoc is stupid, (3) why aoc is a bad leader, (4) why aoc is dangerous, (5) why aoc is terrible, (6) why aoc is against amazon, (7) why aoc is great, (8) why aoc is so important, and (9) why aoc is hate filled.

I couldn't believe the vast difference in suggestions (I think I like *Yahoo!* better). Just for fun, I decided to do the same thing on *Bing*. All I got were suggestions related to air conditioners. So why the stark contrast in suggestions? Biased algorithm.

I did the same thing with "why is democrat..." Here's what I got.

*Google*:

- Why democratic education is important;
- Why democratic socialism works;
- Why democratic socialism is good
- Why democratic leadership is effective

*Yahoo!*:

- Why democrats hate America;
- Why democrat women are wearing white;
- Why democratic socialism doesn't work;
- Why democrats are wrong;
- Why democrats suck;
- Why democrats hate trump;
- Why democrats wear white;
- Why democrats support illegal immigration
- Why democrats lie

My original opinion still stands. I think I like *Yahoo!* better. I didn't even need sources to break this down. If you came to the same conclusion I have, then you know the obvious answer: *Yahoo!* equals honest autofill, while *Google* equals socialist autofill (or something like that). But the bias is obvious I don't need a study to prove it for me.

# 8.

## HYPOCRAT PARTY

AFTER READING THE PAST seven chapters, can anyone honestly come up with a decent argument proving Republicans are racist? Don't bet on it. The Republican Party is made up of at least a 90 percent majority of people who want nothing more than to contribute to our country's prosperity. And those people believe in traditional values.

Have you ever heard the phrase, "Give a man a fish, you've only fed him for the day. Teach a man to fish, and you've just fed him for a lifetime"? Most people have. I always had the understanding that in this world, if you have a goal, you have to put in the effort to get there. The effort won't be put in by someone else. You magically won't succeed. I think the people who know this best are immigrants and conservatives.

I have met immigrants who want nothing more than to succeed in this country. They put in the time to complete the ten necessary steps to becoming a US citizen. Step 1: Check eligibility. Step 2: Complete form N-100. Step 3: Obtain two color photographs of yourself. Step 4: Photocopy documents (including green card). Step 5: Send your application package. Step 6: Get fingerprinted. Step 7: Attend naturalization interview. Step 8: Take English and Civics test. Step 9: Wait for the decision. Step 10: Take the oath.[57] These steps aren't just formalities; they prove you have the qualities of an upstanding US citizen. But there is nothing more that hurts the reputation of legal immigrants than illegal immigrants.

Illegal immigrants are law breakers; it's as plain as that. I know there are likely more well-meaning illegal immigrants than there are ill-meaning ones. There are illegal immigrants hiding in America from drug cartels and those who came to give their children better lives; those are all valid and admirable reasons to come to America. But they need to come in the right way. Just as there are immigrants coming to get away from the cartels, there are also some sent by them as well.

Immigrants are part of American culture, history, and economy. Without them, America wouldn't be America. A study shows that 17 percent of the entire workforce in America is made up of Immigrants.[58] Do you know how huge that is? But there *is* an issue with illegal immigration. A total of 77 percent of immigrants that live in the US are documented and legal, an impressive amount to be sure. But that leaves 33 percent of immigrants to have come in illegally.[59]

What I think Democrats don't understand is how extremely dangerous it is to illegally cross the border. Under Obama, border deaths ranged from 251 to 471 during the years of 2008-2012.[60] There are people who have gone missing in the desert and have never been found. And when I say never found, I mean they vanish almost entirely. What I mean by that is they have died in the desert, and in a time of less than a week, their bodies can be consumed entirely by the desert inhabitants. I won't go into too much detail; suffice to say that desert scavengers aren't at all wasteful. But under Trump's administration, that number had dropped.

There are people called "coyotes" who will smuggle people across border checkpoints. They often charge extremely high prices for families to cross. Some charge as much as $5,000 per person.

There are times when immigrants run into a cartel who will agree to help them cross but only if they become drug mules. And sadly, there are times when entire groups of people are ruthlessly murdered by cartels who'll do the most inhuman and despicable things to them. I absolutely deplore those kinds of people, and that's why I urge immigrants to come in legally, or at the least, wait until they can safely make it.

The border wall was put in place to not only prevent illegal immigrants from coming in but also to reduce the number of migrant deaths. It's a large part of a long-needed immigration reform. For decades, presidents have promised to strengthen border security, and for decades, they have failed to do that. For decades, dangerous drug cartels, like MS-13, have terrorized both legal and illegal migrants, along with American citizens as well.

It's disgusting and sad that the Democratic elitists downplay it. They make it seem as if President Trump believed that *all* immigrants are violent and aggressive, when, in truth, we know it's only a small amount of the illegal immigrants who cross the border that are criminals. In 2019, the DHS reported that out of the roughly 362,000 people intercepted at the US/Mexico border, only 6,259 had criminal convictions. About 800 of those 6,259 had gun-related or violent felony charges. But around 700 of those individuals had ties to violent gangs and cartels.[61]

Democrats have refused to accept there is a problem that needs immediate attention from both political parties. Just look at the thousands of migrants that decided to start heading to America before Biden was even inaugurated. And look how Biden has handled it so far. He handed the issue right over to Kamala Harris, and we all know *her* record of being a compassionate human being. Republicans have had to pick up the slack and go the extra mile.

I care about immigrants; my family is made up of descendants of immigrants from all around the world. Heck, even I was born in another country. If I wasn't adopted, I honestly believe I wouldn't have been given the opportunities I have today.

Republicans care about immigrants; they always have. But immigrants can stand on their own two feet without the help of Democrats who say they are discriminated against. I don't want to hear that I'm xenophobic because anyone who does obviously doesn't know what it means.

These Democrat politicians who call our party a party of xenophobic racists should really read up on their history books. It was FDR who put Jewish refugees into isolated caged-off towns. It was FDR who built internment camps to relocate Japanese citizens.[62] But who was the president who made reparations to the families who had been in these Japanese internment camps? It was Ronald Reagan, a Republican president.

Ronald Reagan signed the Civil Liberties Act in 1988 that would pay back the more than 100,000 families that were wrongly imprisoned. Each surviving victim would receive $20,000, which back then, was the equivalent of $43,000 of today's dollar value.[63] That is just another thing to add to the ever-expanding list of stuff that the Democrats have conveniently forgotten.

Who put in the cages at the border that has been blamed on Donald Trump? Well, Joe Biden will tell you that Obama never locked anyone up at the border. Either Joe forgot, or he's lying again. Obama's administration put in makeshift cages to detain migrant children, and that resulted in the separation of hundreds of children from their families.[64]

During the entire four years of Trump's administration, not once did Obama speak up and say he had put the cages there. If he did, he would have saved a whole lot of division and lies from dividing this country even further. But he didn't because it might have made him look bad and tainted the legacy of his administration.

I can understand people saying that Trump had a stricter immigration policy because comparatively to Joe Biden's flimsy one, he did. What I don't get is why that would make him—conversely Republicans—xenophobic. Wouldn't it be the opposite of xenophobic to do something like that? What happened to America first? What happened to the strength of American manufacturing? What happened to "Made in America"? I'll tell you what happened. All of that was handed off years ago to foreign countries; sold to China, Mexico, and other global manufacturing competitors. But the biggest import that was given away, along with everything else, wasn't physically tangible. It was a portion of the American spirit.

I can understand certain aspects of being a minority. I can understand that certain communities have come a long way in the fight for equality. The Black community has come a long way in a relatively short amount of time. That being said, I can also say that the Black community deserves how far they have come. They worked for centuries being treated poorly. They were mistreated and abused by our country, and for that, I don't think I can ever truly understand what it's like to come from a family with ancestors who were slaves.

But I feel a sense of American pride when I think about just how far minorities have come, how far America has come, and just how far equality has come. I think anyone who says knowledge comes from the color of your skin is a closet racist who has no comprehension of the amount of damage their philosophy truly has on race relations.

There are liberals who think that the national anthem is a form of suppression, so they decided to introduce a "Black" national anthem. Doesn't having two national anthems defeat the purpose of a *national* anthem? Wouldn't that cause more division? Aren't these questions that liberals should have asked *before* kneeling during the national anthem and forcing sporting arenas to play two anthems? Some would argue the national anthem was written by Francis Scott Key, a slave owner, and was written for a country that, for centuries, would allow slavery and thus be a blaring reminder of America's systematic racism.

My argument is, wouldn't the national anthem have more meaning now than ever before because of the triumphs of America? But hey, what do I know? All I am is a believer in America and her citizens. What about that would ever allow me to understand the mistakes America has made? I guess being proud of my country means I have no idea or concept of racism, thus making me a racist White nationalist. If you have faith in America and our system, then you, too, are a racist. Don't try to defend yourself; if you do, you are actually more racist for denying it. The only thing you can do to redeem yourself is to renounce your allegiance to the United States of America and apologize for being White, even if you *aren't* White.

The freedom to practice religion is under attack, and I can tell you it's certainly not by the Republican Party. It's under attack by liberals who believe the Republican majority is made up by disillusioned Christians. And there's nothing worse than a Republican Christian. Apparently, Republican Christians are the ideal kind of humans to spread suppression, oppression, and hate.

Democrats are either scared of Christians or hate them, most likely both. I know they hate Christians because they allow public Bible burnings in cities like Portland, Oregon. If someone burned the Torah, I would consider that to be an anti-Semitic hate crime. If there were organized public Koran burnings, that would fit the definition of an anti-Muslim hate crime. The burning of the holy writings or scriptures of any religion used to fall under the category of religious hate crime.

The Democrats have made a special exception in the case of public Bible burnings. Apparently, Bible burnings are to protest racism. Where is racism in the Bible? Don't liberal activists and Antifa know that from the second the first slave came to the United States, the Pope actually made public objections, saying it was against Christian values? No, they don't remember learning that because they don't bother to learn about what they are protesting.

What I'm about to say next took some time to decide whether or not I should put in this book. But ultimately, tough questions need to be asked. And I truly hope it isn't going to be misconstrued. Why doesn't Antifa burn the Koran to protest the suppression and oppression of Muslim women? Why doesn't Antifa burn the Torah to protest the oppression of LGBTQ? I'll tell you why, it's because they hate America, and it's because they hate what it stands for. If they can take Christianity, the largest religion in the world, out of American culture, they will start the deterioration of every other religion in the US. They don't care about equality or freedom from religious persecution, only destruction.

Most religions have the same moral belief that you should treat others like you would treat yourself. If America becomes a religion-less nation, what would become of any moral compass that keeps this country from going full-on commie? Nothing would stop the Marxists once they destroy the belief of God in America.

Democrat politicians don't stop or denounce public Bible burnings because they know that it only pushes their agenda further. If we allow this to go on for too much longer, America will undoubtedly take a drastic turn to becoming radical-left government. They treat Christians almost as badly as they would in a third-world country.

I never liked the idea of protesters or strikers. I always thought that organizing agitated and sometimes furious crowds could lead to violent situations. That being said, I still support the *right* to protest. I support the right to protest because it's part of free speech. However, in my opinion, a lot of protesters have no idea what they truly are protesting.

How can you call to defund the police in the name of justice when in doing so will just allow dangerous violent criminals to run rampant and go unpunished and uncontrolled? If Black lives mattered to them, why are they burning down not only White-owned businesses but Black-owned businesses? How can they say Republicans are fascists when they continually attack legitimately peaceful Republican protesters, saying they don't have a right to spread their so-called oppressive views.

When I think of Antifa, I see a bunch of costumed losers using the same tactics to "protest" what they claim to be protesting against. If the Democrats don't want to back these people, then maybe there should be a new political party formed. How about a party where Democrats who are hypocrites can spew their nonsensical crap as much as they want? Would the Hypocrite Party be a good name?

You see, you have to practice what you preach, not practice what you preach against. That's not what the Democrat Party has done. They have always been hypocrites, just never this bad. I wish they could be a party I could respect, but I don't; *how can I?* For a party that preaches equality, they sure don't see Republicans as equals, do they? Republicans have always been the underdogs in the game of politics. We have always been lied about, misinformation spread about us, and given an unfair gap to fill in elections.

# 9.

# #CANCELCULTURE

THE BEST PART ABOUT the democrat/liberal culture is the cancel culture; that wonderful instrument they have in their toolbox to get their way. They use it to silence their opponents, punish their enemies, and take down anybody who dares to be different. Don't like the fact that one guy you see on the pillow commercial said something nice about Trump? **Wham**! **Cancel**! Unhappy that the owner of the brand of beans you bought praised the Republican President? **Pow**! **Cancel**! Disturbed that a handicapped actor didn't play a handicapped character in a movie? **Boom**! **Cancel**! Mad that your favorite female country artist was forced to *share* an award with a man? **Ka-pow**! **Cancel the sexist CMAs**!

No one is safe from the wrath of cancel culture, not even dear old granny. It has become a part of our schools, Hollywood, politics, social life, and even business. Cancel culture is a liberal mob technique that is used everywhere and in everything, so beware!

How does cancel culture affect Hollywood and entertainment? Well, in 2020, the classic 1939 movie, *Gone with the Wind*, was taken off HBO Max to protest and denounce racism.[65] What racism? Because there was a Black maid in the movie? But really, it's not because of the maid; it's because HBO was trying to get ahead of the game, trying not to get canceled. It was an appeasement to the liberal mob; they were trying to get the blessings of "woke" activists.

The Black maid in the movie was not some sort of comic-relief Black person, but instead, a different take on a Black woman. The maid from *Gone with the Wind* was a strong, independent, colored woman, which went against the harmful but normalized views of both women and colored people. The actress Hattie McDaniel was actually the first colored woman in history to win an Oscar. While the Oscars had only been around since 1927, it was a shock that a Black woman got an award in 1940.

Ignoring that history, though, is just another way of suppressing Black people and continuing the Democrats' narrative that this country is inherently racist. Wouldn't promoting *Gone With the Wind* and pointing out that the first Black actress to ever win an Oscar was in that movie better and less racially divisive than pulling it? But that doesn't matter; it was bound that, sooner or later, some liberal activist was going to point out that HBO has a movie with politically incorrect content in it, which would lead them to start a movement to get it pulled, followed by going one step further and trying to either sue HBO for racist discrimination or some baseless claims like that or just altogether cancel HBO.

Cancel culture has finally rooted itself deep into our entertainment by becoming a legitimate form of rejection. The Oscars has employed a tactic known as reverse discrimination. Reverse discrimination is the act of favoring a member of a minority group just because they are, in fact, a minority.

The Oscars implemented a rule that for a movie to qualify to win Best Picture, it must meet two out of the requirements from their new inclusion standards. The first standard is that at least one lead role or significant lead role is a member of an "underrepresented" racial or ethnic group. That includes Asian, Hispanic/Latino, Black/African American, Indigenous, and Middle Eastern. The second part of the first requirement is that "at least 30% of all actors in secondary and more minor roles are from two of the underrepresented groups."[66] This includes women, racial or ethnic groups, LGBTQ+, and people with cognitive or physical disabilities, or who are deaf or hard of hearing. The final part of the first requirement is "the main storyline(s), theme or narrative of the film is centered on an underrepresented group(s)."[67] To sum up the first standard, you basically have to make sure your movie is centered around minorities.

The second requirement is, you guessed it, more diversity! The first part of this standard is that either the casting director, cinematographer, composer, costume designer, director, editor, hair stylist, makeup artist, producer, production designer, set decorator, sound, VFX supervisor, or the writer—are made up of at least one racial or ethnic minority and one female, LGBTQ+, or cognitively or physically disabled person. To clarify, make sure you hire somebody because of their identity.

The third standard is, I sound like a broken record, racial or ethnic diversity in the film crew. As I'm sure you can already guess, that includes underrepresented groups, such as LGBTQ+, women, racial or ethnic persons, and someone with a cognitive or physical disability. So basically, the same requirements are as the last standard.[68]

And finally, the last standard is a diverse representation in marketing, publicity, and distribution. *Geez*, if I need to tell you the requirements to meet this standard and you don't already know, then you probably weren't reading this too well.

Now I'm not saying movie producers should be allowed to discriminate, except isn't hiring a person because of their gender, sexual orientation, or racial or ethnic background the same thing discrimination is based upon? Shouldn't someone be hired because of their ability to get the job done and not because you can cross them off on a checklist? I understand and agree there should be diversity in the movie-making process. It would be awfully strange if the credits of a movie were completely made up of the names of straight White men.

Wouldn't a better and less ridiculous way of making sure there is no discrimination is by having an outside, non-biased agent check a movie production to make sure there was no discrimination?

Certain roles have to be played by certain people. Speaking in a logical and historical sense, wouldn't the cast of a movie about Christopher Columbus and the voyage to the new world have to cast Caucasian and Spanish people? Just as a hypothetical, what if, in a movie about the Obamas, Michelle Obama was not played by a dark skinned-woman but rather by a pale red-haired man wearing a wig and dark makeup? How well would that go over? Besides being initially confused, imagine the outrage. Now imagine (hypothetically) if George Washington was not played by a Caucasian man but instead a Cuban transgender woman. There would be *zero* outpouring of public liberal dissent. They would call it the movie of the century. The lead actress would be crowned a trailblazer of Latino LBTQ+ actors and actresses everywhere. Anyone who voices their disagreement would be victimized by cancel culture.

What's the point I'm trying to make? The only thing these guidelines allow to be discriminated against is their stereotypical conception of what the definition of a traditional "overrepresented" American is:

straight, Caucasian, Christian men. While reverse discrimination and traditional discrimination use different tactics, they are both similar in the fact that they cause division, and either way, someone is left feeling cheated.

College *was* a place of diversity, whether it was a diversity of skin color, religion, ethnicity, background, or thought. Apparently, not anymore. Colleges are flaming hotspots for cancel culture and liberal hate to thrive. I cannot stress the amount of hypocrisy and venom that is infused into American universities. Liberal students promote free speech. But at the expense of their peers and professors who make comments they find offensive or politically incorrect, they suppress their voices.

Usually, the "comments" come from average, sensible, everyday people who just want to, like everyone else, have a voice and share their opinions. But, *oh no!* They aren't able to because, like everything else, thought-provoking opinions are offensive, oppressive, and enraging for snowflake liberals.

I'll elaborate. You might say, "I don't think that Kamala Harris would be a strong president." They say, "How dare you say that a woman isn't strong enough to be the president. I hope you and anyone who agrees with you dies! Lol! #lovenothate #blm #stopbullying #antigop." Do you see what I see? If not, then please, please stop reading this book. I really don't know why or how you even got this far.

One tragic example of how far the left takes canceling others is Mike Adams. Mike Adams, who had been the criminology professor at the University of North Carolina in Wilmington for twenty-seven years, became the result of what happens when the liberals go too far with cancel culture.

For years, Adams had been teaching his students while simultaneously exercising his rights as a private citizen of the United States by practicing free speech. He would criticize how the governor handled the coronavirus shutdowns and compared her to a slave owner on social media. Criticizing the government on how they handle things is what Democrats are good at. The only difference between what Mike Adams did and what Democrats do everyday is that Mike Adams was a conservative criticizing a liberal.

Free speech is only free for the left. Republicans pay a price for free speech. What price did Adams pay? He paid with his life.

On July 23, 2020 Mike Adams was found dead in his home.[69] It was eventually determined that he committed suicide by shooting himself. Now why would he shoot himself? He won a court settlement and had the support of thousands behind him, so what would drive a man to do this to himself?

Whether or not liberals realize it or not, words hurt. Just because you have the support of many, even knowing that just one person hates your guts can be devastating. Tens of thousands of raging liberals signed several petitions attempting to ruin the professor's career, using words, such as misogynistic, racist, sexist, xenophobic, vile, and hateful.[70]

So just as a speculation, how many sleepless nights were there leading up to his suicide? How many days were spent crying while being viciously attacked by people who didn't even know him? So if someway a hateful liberal who is guilty of using hateful dialogue to bring down someone else is reading this, know that you need to stop. Words hurt, have consequences, and destroy people.

Even after his death, Adams found no peace. Buzzfeed posted an article the day he was reported dead titled, "A Professor Who Was Known For His Racist, Misogynistic Tweets Was Found Dead In His

Home."[71] Another by NBC was titled, "Professor behind 'vile' racist and sexist tweets found dead in North Carolina home."[72] To be honest, I expected no less from *Buzzfeed*, but I never thought *NBC* would revel in the death of a college professor. It's sick, disgusting, and bigoted.

To the Adams' family, my condolences for your loss. His death, while self-inflicted, was ultimately a modern-day lynching prompted by the liberal's use of cancel culture to make an example of who they considered to be deplorable. This kind of lynching is not based on skin color; it's based on political beliefs. The people who canceled him are his murderers. They are responsible for where they drove him to the edge. They failed at getting him fired, but they feel even better that they got him to commit suicide. They truly are the "pigs" and "bullies" they claim Republicans to be. I don't bully people to stop from speaking their minds. I wouldn't think of ever doing something like that.

How is cancel culture enshrined in politics? Are you told Democrat politicians are fair and honest? If you have been and feel lied to, you probably were misled. Don't believe that nonsense.

If you want a definite example of how Democrats want to cancel political rivals, look no further than Congresswoman Alexandria Ocasio-Cortez (AOC), a loony crackpot liberal with a radical extremist agenda that is the epitome of a communist dictator's wet dream.

AOC tweeted, "Is anyone archiving these Trump sycophants for when they try to downplay or deny their complicity in the future? I foresee decent probability of many deleted Tweets, writings, photos in the future."[73] If that isn't a menacing threat, I don't know what is. That is a call to arms to purge America of Republicans. Shortly after her remarks, the Trump Accountability Project—which has since been shut down—put on its website in agreement to AOC's idea of a "list." "We should not allow the following groups of people to profit from their experience: Those who elected him. Those who staffed his government. Those who funded him."[74]

Ok, you want a list of people who staffed his government and funded him? What about a list of people who voted for him? I won't give it to you. Why? Because I don't speak for those people. But if Democrats want to make a list of the names of the 74,196,153+ people who voted for Trump, then they can take the next—let's see—four... yeah, that's right, *fourteen* years to do that! Make sure half the voter population isn't allowed to work. Let's collapse the American economy. They truly deserve a round of applause for the level of disillusionment they're on (they must be on a new drug). They just won't get it.

Moving right along, besides AOC's "list," we have Democrat news commentator/shock jock, Keith Olbermann, or as he acts, Keith *Goebbels*. This lunatic screams moronic gobbledygook about how much he detests Trump and his supporters. A delirious Keith would love nothing more than a genocide of Trump supporters. The only thing that holds him back from saying that are the particular restrictions of what he can and cannot say on air. Poor Keith has to settle for the next best thing that he is *permitted* to say, to prosecute and destroy the lives of Republicans.

In one of his rants, Keith attempted to start a purging of the deplorable in society; no, not terrorists or Nazis, but instead, Republicans. "He, and his enablers, and his supporters, and his collaborators, and the Mike Lees and the William Barrs...and the Mike Pences, and the Rudy Giulianis and the Kyle Rittenhouses and the Amy Coney Barretts must be prosecuted and convicted and removed from our society while we try to rebuild it and to rebuild the world Trump has destroyed by turning it over to a virus."[75]

His wrath extends an arm to Black people as well. In a deleted tweet, Keith Olbermann attacked Trump using a racial slur. "Yes @realDonaldTrump has always been, will always be, and on the day of his bid for re-election, still is: a whiny little Kunta Kinte."[76] The slur, Kunta Kinte, is used as a derogatory xenophobic, racist term to describe an African immigrant. So why does Keith attack Donald Trump for being racist? I think Keith is more bigoted than he says Trump is. When it comes down to it, Olbermann has always been, will always be, and since the day of his debut as the host of *The Resistance*, still is a whiny snowflake liberal.

Cancel culture only magnifies the hate these people have toward Americans and more. These calls for a list of people who need to be prosecuted and removed from our society sound a lot like what the Nazis did.

Here is what the Nazis did to the Jews: In 1933, there were random attacks on Jews and Jewish properties. The police and justice system began to refuse to protect Jews. Because of Hitler's anti-Jewish propaganda, there were boycotts of Jewish stores and businesses.

One day in April of that year, Hitler told the Germans not to shop at stores owned by Jews. To discourage citizens from shopping at Jewish-run businesses, the Sturmabteilung stood in front of Jewish stores. It was encouraged by the Third Reich to hold public burnings of Jewish and anti-Nazi literature. And the Department of Racial Hygiene, which chiefly meant ethnic cleansing, was established.[12]

The only reason Jews were murdered and hated was that the Nazi party was able to demonize and dehumanize them. They brainwashed the German citizens into believing the things they were told. They controlled where Germans got their information and news. Not to diminish the horrendous atrocities of the Holocaust, but aren't the

Democrats doing the same thing to conservatives? Aren't they dehumanizing and demonizing conservatives?

Isn't Antifa like the SS: undeterred and even promoted by their parent party? The demonization of Republicans by saying they brought our country to ruin—isn't that what Hitler said about the Jews? And encouraging Trump supporters to be identified, refused work, and boycotting conservative businesses is very, very similar to how the Nazis made Jews wear a yellow star of David on their clothes and then discriminated against the entirety of the Jewish population from doing business and refusing to allow them from entering other businesses.

It seems like the Trump Accountability Project had the same basic idea as the Department of Racial Hygiene had of "cleansing." So aren't these Democrats the ones who are supposed to be leaders of their party? Are they truly part of a progressive party? Or are they just a "woke" group of Nazis? It's a slippery slope, and if they aren't careful, they'll sooner become the oppressive fascists.

Social media is one of the worst things that has happened for the development of communication in America, *nay* the world. While it has its pros, I usually only see and hear about its cons. It causes people, especially children and teens, to hyper-focus on what's on their phones. Whether or not a person gets as many likes, views, hearts, or thumbs up on a post as someone else does is a deal of pride now. Imagine what happens when someone not only doesn't get likes but also gets negative comments and a whole lot of hate. On social media, that's how cancel culture works.

When cancel culture is on social media, it's called cyberbullying. You've heard the term before—I know you have. Cyberbullying includes sending messages on social media platforms that are threatening or cruel, intended to harass or belittle someone. I'm sure you have already heard many stories of cyberbullying. When a person is socially canceled, they are excluded from interacting with their peers. Speaking for myself, it doesn't feel too good.

I feel that cancel culture evolved from a system with modest or practical intentions meant to filter what was and wasn't appropriate in public. That system's purpose was to stop violent or obscene gestures and behaviors from being broadcast. Unfortunately, people took matters into their own hands. Whatever *they* deemed to be too vulgar or offensive was either corrected or pulled off the air. Obviously, the first thing that needed to go was political incorrectness, which was replaced by televised sex. They then gave the boot to any actors who made controversial comments. The actors had to be Republican to be kicked off. So thanks to the social justice mob, now TV sucks.

It's kind of funny how Democrats claim to care about women. Here's a list of what you can't do, and it's a pretty reasonable list: no sexist comments, no sexualizing woman, no catcalls, no unwanted advances, and no gender-based salary discrimination. Now here's the part where I give you the unreasonable list the Dems have. So you aren't allowed to sexualize women, right? ***Bam!*** Female sex workers (i.e., strippers, prostitutes) are empowering for feminism, so we need more sex workers. Churches that don't allow female priests? Shut them down! If you say you don't like something about an individual who happens to be a woman (for me, it's Kamala Harris's cackling), you're sexist.

Now, I'm no lady, but how is prostitution empowering? How is stripping feminists? How is selling your body for money a good thing? How is publicly sexualizing yourself not promoting sexist chauvinists? Unless liberals have the ability to stop people who go to strip clubs from sexualizing women and stop pimps from disrespecting prostitutes, I'm pretty sure it's just more B.S.

That's what cancel culture is; more liberal crap meant to inflate the Dems' already bloated ego and sense of self-righteous drivel. It's not fair, it's not honest, and it's sure as heck not true. You don't see me going around boycotting my Democrat teachers. I'm not going to stop watching movies with Johnny Depp just because he's a Democrat. My initial reaction might have been disappointment, but so what? I may only be a teenager, but I'm more grown-up than Rosie O' Donnell. Truthfully, most people are.

# PART TWO

## AGENTS OF CORRUPTION

---

THE PEOPLE WHO MADE this past decade a living nightmare for our country are the same people who poured the mold for the next decade of the Democrat Party. Those people are all close-knit Washington DC swamp monsters, each of whom is of great influence. Bernie Sanders, Barack Obama, Hillary Clinton, Joe Biden, and Kamala Harris are the people who put our country on the track to discontent and corruption. Ironically, each of them has been presidential hopefuls at one point or another in their careers, and all who are tied to Joe Biden and Barack Obama.

Hillary Clinton was the secretary of state when Obama was the president. Joe Biden was Obama's VP. Bernie Sanders, who was a Democrat candidate for the 2020 election, would be and is a strong influence on Biden's policies. Kamala is Joe Biden's VP. Together, they are the spring that fills the Washington swamp. Along with other nasty swamp creatures like AOC, Nancy Pelosi, Chuck Schumer, Ilhan Omar, Cory Booker, Adam Schiff, Amy Klobuchar, and a handful of other Democrat Congress members and senators, they make up the Democrat elites.

While Kamala Harris and Joe Biden hosted virtual town halls with Hollywood and music industry socialites, they pushed their socialist views using the very people we see in our favorite movies. It's a very sick game they play, where they control the media, actors, music artists, activists, and even your social media platforms. Of course, they don't tell you that, but then again, why would they?

To those self-righteous libs, we are just faceless pawns, meant to serve whatever purpose they see fit for us to serve. Our voices don't matter to them unless it helps them out. If your life is ruined by a policy a Democrat politician has made, don't try to petition it by starting a movement. If you do, they'll publicly mock you instead of listening to you. And if they need to be held accountable, they'll just lie, lie, lie, lie, lie, lie, and lie some more to get out of any responsibility (did I mention they lie?). They are the bane of the very ideals that established America. They are the Democrats' agents of corruption.

# 10.

# THE WORST OF THE WORST

THE DEMOCRAT ELITES THRIVE off of the hate in our country, and it's as simple as that. They can take their party's contempt and pin it on anybody and everybody who identifies as Republican. They can take Republicans' discontent with Democratic policies and blame it on Republicans. The Democrats can take any horrible tragedy and accuse Republicans of inciting violence (look at the Vegas shooting and Jan 6, 2020). They did it with coronavirus by blaming Trump for "allowing" it into our country. It never happens to be the fact that they refused to work with the Trump administration to catch it early. And what did they do when rioters burned and looted cities? Who was to blame? Trump was! It couldn't have been their lack of leadership or their calls to defund police, not possibly their direct orders for police to "stand down." So it's completely unfathomable to think it might have been their unwillingness to accept the National Guard from coming in to break up rioters and agitators. So the fact that they allowed rioters and activists to burn down churches and even a police precinct has nothing to do with the overconfident anarchists, right?

Was the fact that the Democrats didn't even bother to lift a finger when statues of Gandhi, MLK, Abraham Lincoln, Theodore Roosevelt,

George Washington, Benjamin Franklin, Christopher Columbus, Thomas Jefferson, and even Jesus Christ were defaced or torn down to be destroyed by violent mobs a contributor to the anarchy? Logic says yes; Democrats say Trump. It doesn't make sense, but that's the Democrat Party for you: "Makes sense to me, but not for thee."

The people who make it their *modus operandi* (big Latin word, I know) to avoid blame by playing a Trump card even in unplayable situations are complete morons. They are the Democrat senators and Congress members who go to Washington, not to be diplomatic, but rather indignant. Some of the worst people up there include Bernie Sanders, Amy Klobuchar, Corey Booker, Kamala Harris, Chuck Schumer, Alexandria Ocasio-Cortez (AOC), Ilhan Omar, and Elizabeth Warren.

All they continue to do is lie, lie, lie, and lie! They have even started to lie to themselves. They are snobbish, annoying, unprofessional, corrupt brats who, if they ever gain complete control of Capitol Hill, will turn it into Capitol Hell! That's why, for your pleasure, I've set up a list of the nonsense that comes from the political left. Whether it's a lie or just plain malarkey, I've put it on the list. *Hey*, just like Alexandria Ocasio-Cortez's "list"!

Senator Elizabeth Ann Warren: She ran (and lost) for the bid of president of the United States in 2020. Running essentially on a promise that she wouldn't be Trump, she tried to be things she wasn't. She tried to claim to be Native American. She had been claiming to have Native American roots for decades. She claimed to be a minority while she was a college professor. She even went as far as to try and run on a minority status. Why? Maybe because it would give her a head start in the Democrat race. She even took a DNA test to prove her oppressed minority status. I guess she was right about being Native

American, though only 1/1,024, right.[77] Yep, she's a Native American, all right.

I have 2 percent Asian ancestry in my blood, but you won't see me filling in any minority boxes. Not because I don't care, but because I just don't think being 2 percent of something makes you that. If Senator Elizabeth Ann Warren's DNA results had instead shown that she was 1/1,024 African American, would she have run as a Black citizen who had to push through years of discrimination to become a senator? It was just another poorly laid foundation for a Democrat candidate to gain a voting block.

I do have to give her credit, though, for apologizing for two decades of false claims. That takes a lot to admit that you were wrong, especially for a Democrat. What's the lesson you should take away from this? Don't announce you are doing a DNA test to prove a point because you might just be wrong. Or perhaps, being cocky can lead to self-publicized humiliation.

Congresswoman Ilhan Omar: She's not pro-American; she's not even progressive. She is a complete and utter anti-American who has shown contempt toward Jews. Her anti-Israel stances have become deafeningly clear in the past few years. While she did endorse Bernie Sanders, who is Jewish, she only did so because of how much his radical agenda aligns with hers.

She hates America so much so that she can barely hide it. On the topic of 9/11, she said, "some people did something."[78] When confronted about her comments, she instead just brought up how she was treated as a suspect after 9/11. Come on, Omar! You're missing the point! It was an attack on American values and American citizens, something that she doesn't seem even to understand or even care about. Yes, Muslims were treated very unfairly in the US after 9/11. But

September 11, 2001 isn't a day to remember religious differences; it's a day to reflect on both the tragedy and heroic actions from that day. You don't care about America; you only care about your agenda.

Ilhan Omar doesn't like Jews. It's as simple as that. She once said that the only reason that the US backed Israel was because of "the Benjamins."[79] She might have as well promoted the outdated anti-Semitic stereotype that Jews are crooked, greedy, hook-nosed schemers, which basically is about the most anti-Semitic stereotype there is. A real role model, people! It's not okay that people stereotype and categorize you after 9/11, but apparently, it's alright to demonize an entire religion because of what? *Your* political agenda? Basically, not only did she shrug off 9/11, she promoted the same harmful rhetoric used to justify the genocide of millions of people. That's sick and disgusting. Oh, and one more thing, just because a person attacks your religion, it doesn't give you the right to do the same back.

Senator Chuck Schumer is an old fart, rude and full of stink, a real Ebenezer Scrooge, to be exact. Like I said earlier in my book, the only reason he sticks to America like gum on the bottom of a park bench is that he needs to stay relevant for him to matter. The only way for him to do that is to become the Democrats' puppy dog. If his super power was encouraging lies and discord, his name would be Captain Chuck Schmuck. And not because he's liberal but because he genuinely is a schmuck.

So to keep himself a prominent politician, he stirs up controversy. It's like the equivalent of a plasma transfusion for him. To keep him chugging on his radical far-left train tracks, he disagrees with anything and everything Republicans have ever attempted to provide a solution to.

Senator Chuck Schumer spread a lie that Trump's tax plan would only benefit the rich and wealthy and stomp on the middle class. According to Politifact,[80] that rumor is full of buffalo chips (excrement). Trump's tax plan would've raised the lowest federal tax rate while essentially increasing the number of people who don't have to pay federal income tax. But thanks to Mr. Schumer, the Democrats have run on the lie that Trump doesn't care about the middle class. Caring about the middle class is what Republicans do. The middle class truly is what makes America great.

Hailing all the way from New Jersey, you know him! You loathe him! You probably couldn't stand his questions at Amy Coney Barrett's confirmation hearings! It's one of America's most polite, snot-nosed, liberal brats! It's Senator Cory Booker! He was raised in a family full of names that start with the letter C, all sounding suspiciously similar; his mother, played by Carolyn Booker, his father, played by Cary Booker, and his brother, also played by a Cary Booker. What's Cory's role? He plays a political pundit whose only connection to any real American is that he was born here! Drained of any real emotions or feelings, this Washington wrestler makes up for it by being great at improv lectures. Cory is his name; lying is his game!

Cory claims to respect women, but does he really? This spectator has reason to speculate on the validity of these claims. In a 1992 column for the Stanford, titled, "So Much for Stealing Second," Cory admits to attempting to take advantage of an underaged intoxicated friend. In the column, Cory Booker compares his sexual advances to a game of chess. He then goes on to say he heard the rhetoric from his friends that "with liquor you get to bed quicker."[81] Was this what was playing in his head as he, at fifteen years old, was thinking? Just because you admit that you groped a woman and it was wrong, that doesn't mean you wouldn't do it again given the chance.

Does Cory really care about women, or is it just a façade? Actions speak louder than words, so words aside, what has Cory done to show he cares about women? I don't remember hearing him condemn Joe Biden for claims of him sexually assaulting a former secretary. More likely than not, Cory wrote about the incident to make himself feel better about what he did.

Her name, you remember, her policies, you forgot before December (2020, that is). Her disposition is about as bright as the Human Torch— if he was scuba diving. She promoted herself as a game changer for America, but really, she was full of hot gas. And everyone heard that hot air when it came out of her lying a—oops, I meant mouth. She's the one, the only, Amy Klobuchar! She does about as much as a pet rock, which is saying a lot. She is a promising package on the outside, and cold, heartless, and disappointing on the inside. To Democrats, she was a promising candidate...because she was a woman; to her staff, a mean old boss-lady.

Posing herself as an anti-Trump to the public, privately to her staffers, she acted, more or less, like Cruella de Vil. Former staffers reported they were berated by their employer, who rained down emails of unprofessional proportions. If Klobuchar thought someone's work was less than par, it was her duty to let them know...from the reasonable window of time between 1 a.m. to 4 a.m. Because there is no better time to give an unprecedented employee review than in the wee small hours of the morning. Mostly over what? Grammatical issues! Misplaced comma here, forgotten letter there. She would call out these world-ending atrocities as what they truly were "The worst (work) in my life."[82] But people don't learn a thing unless you make an example of them. To keep inmates—I mean *employees*—in line, you have to threaten to fire them, usually by an email most likely sent to fellow staff members as well.

If having to endure the modern-day verbal equivalent of being placed in a pillory and having tomatoes thrown at you wasn't bad enough, having actual objects thrown at you is an occupational hazard if you work for Klobuchar! Flying office supplies is the debris that is stirred up during her tirades and tantrums. She once hit a staffer of hers with a binder.[83]

I was hit with a binder once, which resulted in a black and blue thumbnail and a hyperextended thumb. Imagine, if you will, the sheer density of a workplace binder. You could break fingers with a weapon like that!

I'm truly surprised that Amy Klobuchar didn't find a job as an English teacher or prison warden. If she was ever president, she would probably focus more on the interior decor of the White House than international relations! I always thought Klobuchar was a zombie, but when you lose sleep over a missing comma, you're bound to look like death warmed over come morning. I already gave Chuck Schumer a superhero name, why not give one to Klobuchar? I think Senator Shamey Amy is an appropriate alter ego.

I can see it now. Look! Up in the sky! It's a plane! It's a bird! It's Shamey Amy! Crueler than Gordon Ramsey! Even more sarcastic than your mother-in-law! Able to make a fully grown man cry! Sounds like the beginning of the old Superman TV show, right?

I can tell you this, if there ever was a show about Klobuchar, it would be the shortest-running reality TV show in television history! It wouldn't even make it to the second commercial break during the pilot episode! If people wanted to watch a screaming loon, they would just tune in to *Jerry Springer*!

He's the dark knight of deceit, the count of corruption, the peddler of propaganda, and the duke of disinformation. His "facts" are about as real as your grandmother's bowl of wax fruit. It's Adam Schiff! He's in charge to make Trump at large. He may just be another member of what I like to call the "Democrat's Unsubstantiated Made-up Bullcrap," which is just dumb (seriously, it's D. U. M. B.). Besides that, he is also a serious pain in the butt. His Russian collusion theories make him about as credible as a member of the tinfoil hat club. Even *he* knows there is no solid evidence that ties Republicans' 2016 election victory, Russia, and Trump together.

Adam Schiff's lies wasted four years of our lives and taxpayer dollars that will never be seen again. In a desperate attempt to impeach a duly elected president, Schiff had to scrounge around for anything to substantiate his baseless allegations. It was either his reputation or Trump's. It seemed so simple and easy to plant a little bit of dirt on an outsider and political newbie. I mean, how hard can it be to take down someone who has never been a politician before? I guess he screwed that up.

Do you know how upsetting it is to hear that about the Russian collusion hoax? It would be like if Jimmy Kimmel used the same material for over four years (oh, wait, he has), if you had to pay for a movie you didn't even want to see, *or* waiting four hours in a line for the most exciting roller coaster in the world only to reach the front of the line and find out the ride just went out of service. Schiff is a con and hack; he became that when he believed he could convict and impeach a sitting president over a made-up story. I would give Schiff a superhero name, but he's, more or less, like a blobfish; he's just...there, I guess.

All of the people I mentioned *are* the worst of the worst. They lie, distort the truth, propagandize, cheat, demonize, dehumanize, and cover up the truth. Some are worse than others. Some will compare us to rats.

They laugh at us, berate us, humiliate us, dehumanize us, ignore us, despise us, cheat us, attack us, and enrage us. If they cared about equality, they wouldn't do what they continue to do. They do nothing to promote the truth, only their outlooks and agenda.

# 11.

# OBAMA (DID NOT) CARE

BARACK OBAMA WAS ELECTED the president of the United States on November 4, 2008, after beating Republican nominee Senator John McCain. Obama was a fresh, young, (relatively) new politician who made the future of America seem somehow brighter. He represented the beginning of a new chapter in American history as the first non-White president ever.

To America (mostly Dems), he was like the new John F. Kennedy. People loved how he composed himself, his speeches, and his style. He was going to be a president who fought for Americans with his blood, sweat, and tears. He was going to be the president who fought for the Black community. He was supposed to be the president that ushered in a new era.

Well, he was the president who ushered in a new era. Under his administration, he brought the hypocrisy of the Democratic Party to a whole new level. The level of hypocrisy they created is one of no return. It was worse than the level of doggy doo-doo that characterized the Bill Clinton administration. What Obama introduced to Washington DC would lead to Hillary Clinton's Russian collusion hoax scheme, Joe

Biden profiting off the position as vice president, and the rise of Antifa and Black Lives Matter.

When I tell you the things that Obama lied about, you just aren't going to believe what you read. You won't be able to fathom how any one president could do such corrupt things. He is not the great guy everyone thought he was. Behind that smiling face is a typical Democratic politician: selfish and conniving.

Obama is, at heart, an Illinois politician, and true to tradition, a corrupt, phony liar. Chicago is one of the most corrupt cities in America, so it only makes sense that Obama would be too. Barack Obama led this country so poorly that he actually did more harm than good.

Some of Obama's failures as president include the slowest economic recovery in history after coming out of the 2008 stock market crash, Obamacare, North Korean and American relations, he failed to raise the minimum wage as he had promised, and many, many more.[84] How he became president—I can only guess it was the odd pair-up of John McCain and Sarah Palin. How he won a second term, I would appreciate it if someone tossed me a bone on this one because I have no clue whatsoever.

As much as Democrats hail Obama as one of the greatest presidents to ever walk the earth and grace us with his brief heavenly administration, Republicans think exactly the opposite. Who's right? Most Republicans will tell you that Obama just piled onto an already huge mound of issues plaguing our country. *Sure*, Obama had a few upstanding moments, but that doesn't make him America's savior.

I don't think that just because he is African-American automatically means he did the most ever for the Black community. I would go as far as to say that he did nothing whatsoever. To me, all it seems he did was take some photo-ops of himself with activists. If White people can harm White people, then Black people can harm Black people; it's not about skin color. So in my opinion, I think he honestly is one of the most overrated presidents of all time. I mean that in the most honest and fair way possible. What's the big hype? Besides being the guy in office when Bin-Laden was finally done away with, what lasting impact did he have on our country?

I'll give him credit, though; no American president has ever had their spouse become more idolized than them after leaving office than Obama did. Because while a few came close, Michelle Obama got a freaking Grammy, and for what, an audiobook of herself narrating the book she wrote?[85] If I narrated this book—if you want to call it that—in an audiobook, would I win an award? If I played myself in a movie adaptation of this book, would I win Best Actor at the Oscars?

I used to respect Michella Obama. That was when she used to stand for something. Now she has become an insulting media personality who, for some reason or other, is consulted to comment on things she probably has no previous knowledge or comprehension of.

The only thing that came out of Obama's administration that lasted was that more corrupt politicians who want to be the president became part of our government. Frankly, that is something America was already full of. But like I've said before, what do I know? Maybe covering for your vice president's role in their son's corrupt business deals overseas is an admirable trait in a president. I never thought that hiding the fact that your secretary of state, who happens to be a candidate for the presidency, is trying to stir up a fake investigation into one of her political opponents to distract from their own deleted subpoenaed emails was something people look up to, but I guess times are changing, right?

I think it's cute that four years after Obama left office, only just now, we're just discovering the horrible secrets his administration had kept. I thought we learned our lesson after George W. Bush; guess not. Not just that, these are things a certain golden-haired billionaire made allegations about for years. I guess that guy wasn't so crazy after all. Funny how things like that work out. Maybe the media will do actual reporting next time something like this happens. Then again, that's about as plausible as a Bernie Sanders 2024 campaign for president.

Obama made many mistakes in his administration, but none as bad, sneaky, and low as when he hid the fact that Hillary Clinton was trying to ruin Trump's chances of becoming president. When former CIA Director John Brennan had briefed the president, Barack Obama automatically became an accomplice in the phony investigation into allegations of Trump colluding with the Russians to help him win the election. Thanks to the director of National Intelligence, information pertaining to the hoax was released. The info was more incriminating than a pool of blood left at a scene of a crime by the culprit. This was Obama's Watergate.

John Brennen's note, which was declassified, revealed that Obama had been briefed on a "plan" cooked up by then-presidential hopeful Hillary Clinton to plant disinformation on Donald Trump. The disinformation she would sow was that—and you all know the story, so all together now—the Trump campaign colluded with Russian intelligence. Now I'm not saying Obama was a participant of Hillary Clinton's plan. But since he did nothing to stop her *or* debunk or expose her, he is then an accomplice, along with John Brennon.[86]

Obvious similarities between Obamagate and Watergate, eh? Richard Nixon wasn't directly responsible for the Watergate Complex break-in, though he had been briefed on it and had been responsible for its cover-up. Conversely, Barack Obama wasn't directly responsible for the disinformation that came from Hillary Clinton, though he had been briefed on it and had been responsible for its cover-up. So on that level, that makes Obama and Nixon equally corrupt presidents.

What pushes Obama ahead of Nixon on the Corrupt-O-Meter? Well, perhaps a second cover-up will do it. Obama probably knew about Joe Biden's role in his son, Hunter Biden's, overseas business deals. While there is no direct evidence suggesting Obama knew about Joe, Hunter, and China, it's a matter of time before there is. We already know Obama knew about Joe's position on Burisma in Ukraine. Just look at the facts! Let's go over what we know in general.

A. Joe Biden was Obama's vice president;

B. Hunter Biden is then-Vice President Joe Biden's son;

C. Joe Biden used Air Force Two to fly both him *and* his son to China; and

D. Around that time, Hunter had begun doing business with China.

Anybody who does their research can tell that Hunter Biden is not a businessman. You do the math.

Let's do a little role-playing. Let's see what *might* have transpired between the big O and the little J.

Obama: "Hey Joe, you're flying out to China today, are you planning on bringing anybody special?"

Biden: "Yeah, besides Jill, I'm bringing my son, Hunter!"

Obama: "What for?"

Biden: "Oh, you know, man, sightseeing, family time, business. The usual stuff."

Obama: "Business? I didn't know your son was a businessman."

Biden: "He's not. So I'm giving him a hand by 'weighing' in with my position. What use is being vice president if you can't use it to help yourself and your family out, right?"

Obama: "You have got a valid point there. Just make sure this never becomes a conflict of interest. It might get you and me into unnecessary trouble."

Obviously, I made that conversation up. *But,* it seems plausible, especially if you read it with their voices in your head. Seriously, how could Obama *not* have known?

What we *do* know Obama knew of was business deals the Bidens had in Ukraine. In an eighty-seven-page report of a probe led by the GOP, it's outlined that Obama was informed on the subject and that it was a "conflict of interest."[87] A direct excerpt from the report—which I obtained from the *Wall Street Journal*—summarizes it pretty clearly:

On April 16, 2014, Vice President Biden met with his son's business partner, Devon Archer, at the White House. Five days later, Vice President Biden visited Ukraine, and he soon after was described in the press as the "public face of the administration's handling of Ukraine." The day after his visit, on April 22, Archer joined the board of Burisma. Six days later, on April 28, British officials seized $23 million from the London bank accounts of Burisma's owner, Mykola Zlochevsky. Fourteen days later, on May 12, Hunter Biden joined the board of Burisma, and over the course of the next several years, Hunter Biden and Devon Archer were paid millions of dollars from a corrupt Ukrainian oligarch for their participation on the board.[88]

The report later says that the "Obama administration knew that Hunter Biden's position on Burisma's board was problematic and did interfere in the efficient execution of policy with respect to Ukraine.[89]

I don't know how much clearer it can be. Obama knew about Joe Biden's position on the Burisma board, but he didn't address it. That sounds pretty crooked to me. So we know of two high-profile corrupt things Obama did: Obamagate and Bidengate. I sincerely and non-sarcastically hope Obama didn't do anything else *that* corrupt, for the Democrats' sake. One cover-up is bad enough, two should raise some serious doubts, but three might just be pushing the envelope a little too far.

Obama was a failure; he couldn't get his own party together. That's why nothing ever got done while Obama was in office. Congress was made up of a majority of Democrats during the first half of Obama's first administration, yet somehow, *they* couldn't agree on policies.

Obama promised a lot, but he gave only very little. He broke promises, and the ones he broke were the ones he probably should have focused on. Here are some of the promises he failed to keep, courtesy of *PolitiFact*:

- He never doubled American exports as he told us he would;
- He wasn't able to "create a new tax credit for companies that bring jobs to the United States from overseas";
- He failed to fulfill his promise to "create 1 million new manufacturing jobs by the end of 2016";
- He failed to "provide a path to citizenship for undocumented immigrants"; and
- End the war in Afghanistan in 2014? Yep! He was unable to do that (and before the end of his administration, ironically, he increased the quantity of troops overseas).[90]

Obama failed to better America; it's obvious. I don't say that out of spite. I say that because just by looking at the major mistakes and broken promises he made during his administration, it's obviously an accurate statement. Just looking back, I remember a lot of Republicans voted for Obama in 2007. Many ended up regretting it. All I can say in his behalf is that he was a strong speaker, very enthusiastic, and was "positive." Obama's legacy? Corruption, lies, cover-ups, and let-downs. Obama could have been a great president. He failed.

# 12.

## HILLARY (AND BILL)

### (A VERY, *VERY* SUS COUPLE)

WHO COULD BE THE perfect match for Bill Clinton? Who was somebody he could have a troubled marriage with? Who would be able to berate and attack women just as much as he sexualized them? Who is someone who is lean, mean, possibly a heartless political machine? Who is someone who can lie better than Bill? Why, try Hillary Clinton, of course!

Hillary Diane Rodham Clinton was born at the Edgewood Hospital in Chicago on October 26, 1947, to Hugh and Dorothy Rodham. Being part of an upper-middle-class family, Hillary had a generally "comfortable" childhood growing up in Parkridge, a suburb of Chicago. She was able to attend both Wellesley College *and* Yale University. At Yale, she met her future husband (and co-conspirator), Bill Clinton. In 1975, they were wed, and five years later, their daughter, Chelsea, was born. From 1979 to 1981, Bill served as the governor of Arkansas after serving his term as the attorney general from 1977-1979. He wasn't able to serve two consecutive terms as governor, so he ran again in 1982, won, and was sworn-in in 1983. He ran a third and fourth time in 1984 and 1986 for re-election.[91]

People often tell you to separate work-life from home-life. For politicians, they would recommend that you keep your children protected from the world of politics. Even political opponents respect this unspoken rule. Attacking a political figure's child/children, especially if they are underage, is unprofessional, inappropriate, cheap, and, not to mention, classless. For the Clintons, they didn't need to have some outside critic expose their daughter to the world of cruel politics; they were capable of doing that just fine themselves.

In an August 31st, 1998 article from *Time* magazine, Hillary Clinton admitted to having deliberately made her daughter, Chelsea, cry in an attempt to make her tough. Chelsea was six at the time when her father ran for re-election as governor of Arkansas in 1986. Of course, Bill, being a busy governor, understood the value of a mirthful childhood. He *should* have made sure to protect his daughter from the kind of world he faced every day. He did value giving his daughter one thing he never had growing up: an irrationally mean and selfish father (because he didn't grow up with one). While most normal parents taught their children the facts of life and bought them pet rocks, the Clintons played pretend media harassment with Chelsea pretending to be Governor Bill Clinton and Bill and Hillary playing the vicious media.[1]

I'm sure that if you called me a fascist, I would be offended and angered. If you called me that when I was six, I would just give you a quizzical look and go back to watching SpongeBob and sipping my milk through a chocolate-flavored straw (you know the one I mean). So what would you say to upset a six-year-old girl? If I had to guess, it would be a loser, dumb, stupid, liar, cheater, ugly, tattletale—the basic stuff.

Chelsea's parents would have her make "speeches" to why people should vote for her, only to attack her by saying harsh things. But since compassion isn't this odd couple's forte, what they did seemed perfectly normal. In Hillary Clinton's eyes, she succeeded as a mother. Since Hillary has no visible emotions besides cockiness and smugness, it would only make logical sense that Chelsea inherits that trait. The Clintons' unusual parenting tactics worked! "She gradually gained mastery over her emotions," Hillary would go on to say.[92]

In June 1995, a twenty-five-year-old Monica Lewinsky began her unpaid internship at the White House. She quickly became "acquainted" with President Clinton and how to best "serve" him. In November 1995, Monica and Bill began a secret sexual relationship that would last two years and consist of fourteen "interactions." I read the report and was so shocked by what I heard; all I can say is that it involved a cigar, a blue dress, and secret audiotapes. I can only suppose that Bill Clinton brought a new meaning to "under the desk corruption."

What has Hillary done since then? She has tried to pick up the Clinton family name's fractured reputation, trying too hard to forget what had happened. Now I'm not saying Hillary Clinton deserved what her husband did to her. Nobody deserves that, but instead of making the incident a learning moment, she took nothing away from the experience whatsoever. I'll explain why.

Since Lewinski, multiple allegations against Bill Clinton have been made, four in particular. These allegations are serious and should be treated as such. Sure, I feel a tinge bit bad for the Clinton family, but he should be held accountable if Bill did something wrong.

The first allegation came from Juanita Broddrick, initially in 1999. She said that in 1978, while Bill Clinton was still the attorney general in Arkansas, she had met him in a hotel room on a campaign stop. Broddrick, who was thirty-five at the time, was a nursing home administrator. When she met with Clinton, she expected the encounter to occur in a hotel coffee shop in Little Rock. Broddrick's allegations then go on to say that rather than meeting in the coffee shop, Bill Clinton instead suggested they meet in her hotel room. Once they got there, Bill Clinton raped her.[93]

You may be wondering why she didn't bring up the allegations earlier. Well, intimidation can work wonders. Just weeks after the alleged rape, Juanita Broddrick attended a Clinton political rally in Van Buren, Arkansas. While at the rally, Broddrick was approached by Hillary Clinton. Hillary grabbed her hand and, with a "friendly" smile, said, "I am so happy to meet you. I want you to know that we appreciate everything you do for Bill." When Broddrick tried to pull away, Hillary just squeezed tighter, reiterating her point, "Everything you *do* for Bill."[94] Disgusting. Of course, this is just an allegation, meaning that Bill Clinton has never been convicted of raping Juanita Broddrick.

When Juanita tried to detail the incident to NBC, two producers refused to let her talk about it.[95] It's just another example of liberal bias in the media.

A second incident—which did result in justice of sorts—details how Bill Clinton descended upon Paula Jones. In 1991, Paula Jones, an Arkansas state employee at the time, attended a government quality-management conference. A state police officer had informed her that Clinton wanted to meet her, so she followed him to Clinton's hotel room in Little Rock. In an interview with Paula Jones, she recalls the incident of what happened when she got to his room. "He sat down, pulled down his pants, his whole everything, and he was exposed, and I said, 'I'm not that kind of girl, and I need to be getting back to my desk.'"

Once she tried to leave, Clinton blocked the door and gave her a slimy remark, "You're a smart girl—let's keep this between ourselves." When she left, the officer who had brought her there, was standing outside of the door "smirking."[96]

Unlike Juanita Broddrick, Paula Jones accused Bill Clinton in 1994 and brought a sexual harassment lawsuit with her. Unfortunately, in 1998, a federal judge dismissed the lawsuit explaining that Jones had neither proof nor evidence that the incident harmed her or her career. I don't get what about exposing yourself isn't sexual harassment? Jones appealed the ruling, and Clinton had to pay $850,000 in an out-of-court settlement agreement. To save face, Bill Clinton never admitted to any wrongdoing or apologized in any way.[97]

How did Hillary play a role in this? Well, to begin, she tried to get several lawyers to spread rumors of nude photos of Jones *and* subpoena men in an attempt to uncover "evidence" of the incident. Even *Politico* agrees that while the allegations were "dubious," they happened to still be "credible."[98]

Another allegation against Bill Clinton came from Kathleen Willey, who was sexually assaulted by Bill in the Oval Office. During Bill Clinton's campaign in 1992, Kathleen Willey and her husband donated thousands to his cause. In 1993, Kathleen was a volunteer at the White House. But to her, it seemed that she and Bill were more than acquaintances; she had the impression that they were "good friends." When Bill Clinton became the president in 1993, Kathleen Willey worked as a volunteer in the correspondence office, where she would help go over and reply to the mail that would come to him. At no point before the incident did Mrs. Willey give or get the impression that they were anything more than friends

Kathleen received a phone call after coming home from the traditional White House Easter Egg Roll from Nancy Hernreich, the White House director of Oval Office operations. Apparently, the president had an interest in her "working someplace else other than correspondence." Kathleen Willey was ultimately moved to an office closer to Clinton's and would then see more of the president.

Kathleen's husband, Ed Willey, was a lawyer who was in deep trouble for embezzling money from his clients, causing them to be in financial distress. Kathleen was still a volunteer at the time, but she needed to get a paying job to help her husband and family. She told her husband that she was going to Washington to ask the president for a full-time paying job.

She came to Bill, distressed and distraught. Clinton seemed to be sympathetic to her cause, even going as far as to offer her a cup of coffee. He agreed to do everything he could to help her out. But before Kathleen could leave, Bill gave her an unusually long hug. No red flags were raised initially until Clinton began to kiss her on the mouth and grope her. Kathleen pushed away and decided to leave. Being a donor of the president, Kathleen worried about the repercussions of what would happen if she came forward. It wasn't until 1998 when Bill was in hot water for the Monica Lewinsky affair, would she step forward.

How did Hillary play a role in this situation? Well, the president's personal attorney at the time, Mr. Bennett, who had worked with Hillary to intimidate Paula Jones, was also on the case to intimidate Kathleen Willey as well. It can only lead me and others to point out that Hillary Clinton had to have been involved in or even at least have been aware of Bob Bennett's pressuring of Kathleen Willey.[99]

The fourth allegation comes from Leslie Millwee. Bill Clinton assaulted her when he was still the governor of Arkansas, and she was a television reporter. Millwee worked under the name of Leslie Derrick at the time and had interviewed Mr. Clinton on multiple occasions. On three occasions, Bill Clinton would pack into the small editing room where Millwee was working so he could secretly "fondle" and "grope" her. The second time Clinton sexually harassed her, he tried to become more "intimate." Each time, she rejected his advances only to be laughed at by him. One day, Clinton tried to persuade her to let him into her apartment. When she refused, he left. Eventually, the abuse and harassment were too much, and she quit her job at the television station.[100]

How did Hillary intimidate her? To be honest, there is nothing that directly ties Hillary to attempts at pressuring her. But Hillary has attempted to discredit her along with the other women. I'm sure Hillary didn't know about each and every time Bill sexually assaulted women. But she *had* to have thought that these women, at the very least, would destroy her husband and any political aspirations she had if they were believed. Hillary Clinton tried to play the victim card herself when Donald Trump called her a "nasty woman."[101] She had "nasty woman" t-shirts printed out for women. She tried to frame that as how Trump felt about all women. Hillary truly is a nasty person.

So much for #MeToo. What's the point of seeking justice when it's one-sided? At the 2020 Democratic National Convention, speakers, such as Barack and Michelle Obama, Jimmy Carter, Hillary Clinton, and other notable figures were in attendance. The one that surprised me the most was Bill Clinton. We all know what Bill was going to do, talk about Trump's failures and Biden's successes. What I didn't see coming was Bill accusing Trump of misconduct in the Oval Office. I don't need to write a whole paragraph on how dumb that sounds coming out of Bill's mouth. You don't need to read a whole paragraph on how dumb it sounds. We all know how dumb it sounds. So I'll give you a one-word sentence we all can agree on to sum up Bill's DNC speech: hypocrisy.

In 2016, Hillary Rodham Clinton lost the presidential election. I and millions of others will tell you that she lost because that's how the electoral college works. People didn't trust her. She was never meant to be the president. But Hillary knows what happened. The only logical and reasonable explanation is that it was Russia! Yes! Russia and Donald Trump must have been in cahoots with each other to hack the voting system.

Her theory was and still is so incredibly plausible to the desperately frantic Democrats that, despite the total and utter complete lack of evidence to support it, it's used to explain what happened in 2016. It's used to explain every technical issue to date! Did somebody hack into the US treasury? It must have been Russian hackers! Trump must have asked Russia to hack into the treasury to help him take back the election! Nevermind that the treasury has nothing to do with elections whatsoever! Yeah, thanks for your take on current issues, *CNN* and Jake Tapper.

What we *do* have evidence of is Hillary Clinton's use of a private email to share **classified** documents. Yeah, **big** no-no. Hillary Clinton once even criticized Bush for his administration's use of non-governmental email servers. I won't go into the nitty-gritty of the details of the Clinton email scandal (Emailgate?). It would take me an entire book to do that. Instead, I'll give you a quick run-down of what happened.

Hillary had emails; some were official *classified* emails, and some were casual inconsequential emails. Those emails were circulated through her own private email servers. On March 4, 2015, Hillary

Clinton received a congressional subpoena from the House Select Committee on Benghazi. The subpoena, in no uncertain terms, stated verbatim, "For the time period of January 1st, 2011 through December 31, 2012, any and all documents and communications in your possession, and/or sent from or received by the email addresses 'hdr22@clintonemail.com,' 'hrod17@clintonemail.com,' or any other email address or communications device used by you or another on your behalf, referring to or relating to:

A. Libya (including but not limited to Benghazi and Tripoli);
B. weapons located or found in, imported or brought into, and/or exported or removed from Libya;
C. the attacks on U.S. facilities in Benghazi, Libya on September 11, 2012 and September 12, 2012; or
D. statements pertaining to the attacks on U.S. facilities in Benghazi, Libya on September 11, 2012 and September 12, 2012."[102]

Seems pretty clear, *right?* Apparently, it was not clear enough for Clinton.

Three weeks after receiving the subpoena, 33,000 emails were deleted. I would say it was a scrubbing of her servers in an attempt to try and erase any culpability Clinton may have had for the resulting attack in Libya, leaving four American citizens and an ambassador dead. The subpoena was released by Trey Gowdy after Hillary claimed she had never received a subpoena. When confronted, her line of defense was that the emails were private and personal.

To divert attention from herself, Hillary Clinton stirred up a hoax that has lasted since 2016, a hoax that began the longest witch hunt against a sitting president in US history and cost millions of taxpayer dollars; a hoax that you and I both know. The Russian collusion hoax began in late July 2016, when Hillary Clinton approved a proposal from one of her foreign policy advisors. The proposal was aimed at vilifying Republican presidential candidate Donald Trump by tying the Trump campaign to interference conducted by Russian security services. It alleged that billionaire Donald Trump was in hijinks with Russian President Vladamir Putin and the Russian hacking of the Democratic National Committee.

Now I know it sounds like I copied, pasted, and edited the story of the Watergate scandal, but I didn't. This is the best that Hillary's staff could come with. Their story was like a Chinese bootleg rip-off of a popular movie. Like *Chop Kick Panda* and *Ratatoing* (which are actual crappy rip-offs), the Russian hoax should have been just as obvious.

Somebody the Democrats placed their bets on was Robert Mueller. Mueller was the one who would pin irrefutable evidence of collusion on Trump. He was, in no uncertain terms, a bumbling tool. When he testified and gave his carefully revised report with redactions, the evidence was unbearable, overwhelming, and just, just...completely lacking! What the Democrats had received was about as revealing as a nudist wearing a trenchcoat. But it was all there, anything and everything the Democrats needed to reassure them Trump did nothing wrong. But the proof wasn't good enough. To them, Trump was a bad, bad man; he *had* to have done something illegal. He didn't, not during the election, and not after either.

Well, it's good to know that the Hillary campaign was the only group of people to be complicit. I'm so glad that if anybody had known outside of Hillary's little duck pond, they would have exposed the lie. Oh, *wait...*Smack!* Barack Hussein Obama knew. He knew months prior to the election. But how could *he* have known?! Perhaps a note written by the former CIA director John Owen Brennan (J. O. B.) briefing Obama on the plan does the trick. It is also suspected that James Comey was there since his initials, J. C., were on the note. Who else could J. C. stand for? Jim Carey? James Corden?

The note is not vague, at least not the parts that relate to the hoax. The note relating to Clinton shows that Hillary gave her approval to vilify Trump or at least reason to believe Clinton approved a plan to vilify Trump:

We're getting additional insight into Russian activities from [REDACTED]...CiTe alleged approved by Hillary Clinton a proposal from one of her foreign policy advisers to vilify Donald Trump by stirring up a scandal claiming interference by the Russian security service.[103]

Wouldn't that have been nice to know? That may have sped up a grueling year's-long investigation. But hey, Obama's a smart guy. He knew that if this had become public information, an investigation into his presidency might ruin his tropical island retirement.

When James Comey was asked whether he received an investigative referral, he responded with, "doesn't ring any bells with me."[104] That's an answer he carefully worded, you can count on it. His answer makes it either a denial of ever receiving a referral *or* if it turns out he did get a referral, he just doesn't remember. That answer possibly gave him reason to say he never lied about receiving it, just that he couldn't remember receiving it. Just a side note, this is a guy who supposedly remembers Trump supposedly discussing a "golden showers" tape that Putin supposedly had.[105] Yeah, trust a guy like that.

It would be nice if Hillary came forward and admitted there was no discussion of Trump and Russian interference until someone on her campaign suggested it. But there's about as much of a chance of that happening as there is of me not publishing this book; So basically, not a chance.

# 13.

## SLEAZY JOE

JOSEPH ROBINETTE BIDEN JUNIOR was born on November 20, 1941, in Scranton, Pennsylvania. His mother was Catherine Eugenia Finnegan; his father was Joe Biden Senior. I won't go over Biden's entire background too much because I have fifty years of lies to go over. I will address his racism, sexism, and role in his son's overseas business deals. Let's dive in.

**Racey Joe**: Joe Biden has, on multiple occasions, claimed he was going to "divert" funding away from the police.[106] But that's just him doing what he does best: giving into the radical left. It comes as no surprise that Joe promised a **lot** of things during the campaign that he won't be able to keep. He can't "ban" fracking. He went back and said he would "transition" out of fracking and planned to have America 100 percent energy efficient by 2050.[107] If you take a look at what he said, he basically admitted he'll do something that'll have results thirty years from now. I'm sure he doesn't plan on being alive by then, so who's to blame (probably conservatives)? But that's not the point. The point is that Joe Biden has said whatever he feels is necessary to help him out.

Joe Biden paints himself as a guy who feels guilty of America's racist past; I call malarky. In 1970, when Joe Biden served his first year as a senator, he had a commonly conservative opinion on reparations: "I don't feel responsible for the sins of my father and grandfather. I feel responsible for what the situation is today, for the sins of my own generation, and I'll be damned if I feel responsible to pay for what happened 300 years ago."[108] Now, it's not racist to have that opinion, but I'm just pointing out his hypocrisy. Now I wonder why he changed his rhetoric? Perhaps it's because of who he hung around—namely former Senator Robert Byrd.

Robert Byrd was from a time when Democrats were racist, and Republicans, most of whom were (and still are) not. Byrd was a member of the Ku Klux Klan, a Cyclops, to be exact, in his younger days. What were his thoughts on Black people? "I shall never fight in the armed forces with a Negro by my side. Rather I should die a thousand times and see Old Glory trampled in the dirt never to rise again, than to see this beloved land of ours become degraded by race mongrels, a throwback to the blackest specimen from the wilds."[109] That's from a letter he wrote in 1944. A very cheery disposition that Senator Byrd had.

In 1964, twenty years later, Senator Byrd filibustered the Civil Rights Act for fourteen hours. You have to be tremendously dedicated to oppose something like that for fourteen hours. He even opposed the nomination of Thurgood Marshall to the Supreme Court in 1967. But once again, I am inclined to point out that it seems as if he drastically changed his stance on Black people later in his career. When Robert Byrd died in 2010, Joe Biden gave a eulogy. To him, Byrd was a "guide," "mentor," and "friend".[110]

Joe Biden is either a racist or just doesn't care about racial equality as much as he says he does. Every now and then, Biden lets slip a subtly racist remark. It wouldn't be fair if I didn't back up that claim without any proof. So I found several questionable comments Joe Biden has made. In 1977, Biden said he didn't want his kids to grow up in a "racial jungle." Here's what he said: "Unless we do something about this, my children are going to grow up in a jungle, the jungle being a racial jungle with tensions having built so high that it is going to explode at some point."[111] To me, it sounds as if he's afraid his kids are going to grow up in a racially diverse and racially tense world. Well, thankfully we *do* live in a racially diverse country because of average people; unfortunately, it only continues to become more and more tense.

Joe Biden served as the vice president under Barack Obama, the *first* Black president. But to Joe, his running mate Obama was "the first mainstream African American who is articulate and bright and clean and a nice-looking guy. I mean, that's a storybook, man."[112] Joe likes to make facts up. I mean, he thinks that a Black man invented the lightbulb—or at least that's what a staffer probably told him to say. But it seems as if Joe forgot that the abolitionist, Fredrick Douglass, was nominated as the vice president for Victoria Woodhull, who was an equal rights suffragette. Frederick Douglass is somebody *all* Americans can admire. To me, Fredrick Douglas was one of the most significant voices in the abolition of slavery and equal rights. Tragically, he goes under-appreciated. Yes, Obama was polished, yes Obama was articulate, and yes Obama was relatively bright. *But* he was far from the first.

Joe Biden spent a lot of time down in his basement last year shielding himself from the campaign. Initially, I thought it was because he didn't want to make any gaffes or racist comments. But Joe doesn't like rumors, so he gave us the *real* reason he was acting like it was the Cold War era and his basement was a nuclear fallout shelter: Black women. Joe believes that "the reason I was able to stay sequestered in my home is because some black woman was able to stack the grocery shelf."[113]

Let's pretend it's the 1850s and we're in the Deep South. Joe Biden is running for president. He's making an argument on why slavery is essential to Southern progress. What would his argument be? "The reason I was able to stay financially stable is because some black woman was able to pick the cotton on my plantation." Do you see what I mean?

I already told you about Joe's "you ain't black" and his "more diverse than the black community" comments, so why is he *not* a racist? *He's not Trump*, explains Democrats. But Biden's inner circle doesn't truly believe he's woke. Kamala Harris thinks Biden is a racist; she said so during a debate. But now that she's vice president, she doesn't think that anymore. Kamala sucks up to Joe Biden now that she's one heartbeat, or in her case, one gaffe away from the highest office in the land (and she knows it and hopes it).

The Joe Biden Democrats see is so much different from the actual Biden. When Joe Biden was inaugurated, I decided to give him a grace period. That meant I would try my best to allow him a month in office before judging his administration for the next three years and eleven months. Believe me, folks, I tried, truly I did! I even was able to make it longer than all of the conservatives I know. I made it at most twelve hours! Unfortunately, he signed several executive orders that showed just how "unifying" and "moderate" he truly is.

Joe Biden is a liar and hypocrite. What's the difference between a liar and hypocrite? Well, for starters, when you say you are going to be the most blue-collar president in American history, but then destroy 11,000+ pipeline construction workers' livelihoods as one of your first executive orders—and then, to add insult to injury, tell them to go and make solar panels—you're a liar. Knowing Biden, he probably thought being the most blue-collar president meant having a closet full of blue-collar shirts. When you claim to support unions but the only union you seem to support is the teacher's union, you're a liar. Those are the actions that describe a liar.

Now a hypocrite is a person whose philosophy is to do as one says, not as one does. A hypocrite is the kind of person who'll tell you to love all people but also explains that a quarter of the nation (all of whom don't like that person) belong to a basket of racist, sexist, homophobic, xenophobic, Islamiphobic "deplorables" (I'm talking to you, Hillary Clinton). When you say that only a dictator would use executive orders to fulfill their agenda but then sign fifteen executive orders on the first day of your administration, you're a hypocrite. When you choose a female vice president in a move that supposedly empowers women but then destroys women's sports by allowing biological men who identify as female to compete in their division, you're a hypocrite. Besides denying the biological differences (which is also science you should follow, Joe), it's kind of bigoted if you think about it.

What do the actions say about what they really think? Sure, women have come a far way, and along the way, have achieved so many inspiring and amazing feats, so we shouldn't blur their accomplishments with those of men. That being said, if an individual who was born as a male but now identifies as a woman feels compelled to win a gold medal in women's boxing, his victory should be seen as an achievement for all women (except for the one he just sent to the hospital with brain damage).

What exactly am I trying to convey about Joe Biden? What I'm trying to say is that Joe Biden is a liar. What you know is that he's a hypocrite. To put it simply, the "Legend of Joe Biden" is just that, a legend, myth, fable, tall tale, fallacy, fantasy, illusion, mirage, and bedtime story told to comfort liberals. Joe Biden is all smoke and mirrors. "Look at all the minorities he placed in his cabinet!" they exclaim while they rush a cognitively struggling Joe Biden away from the press. Honestly, they could have a malfunctioning animatronic from the Hall of Presidents at Disney World and say it's Joe Biden, and we would probably buy it.

**Sleepy Creepy Joe**: Joe Biden, like the rest of us, has bad habits. For some people, it's picking their nose. For others, it's biting their fingernails. For Joe, it's smelling female hair follicles. Maybe Joe isn't a creep; perhaps he just likes the scent of Nexxus Humectress Ultimate Moisture Conditioner. But I likely doubt it, considering he's a dirty old man. Joe Biden has, on countless occasions, embraced women inappropriately.

When confronted, Biden explains that he feels it's important to make connections. The mainstream media responds with, "We can buy that." It's about as shallow as Bill Clinton explaining his sexual affair with Lewinsky was to help him deal with stress.

It wouldn't matter if Joe Biden were to have a press briefing on the birds and the bees. The whole situation would undoubtedly be framed as "America's favorite uncle discusses the facts of life with adoring children nationwide." Honestly, it seriously would not matter to the media if Joe Biden began to regale the entire nation with stories of children rubbing the hair on his legs. They wouldn't even cover it up; they would spin it as a positive thing.

What indeed strikes me as warped is that out of all the women who alleged Trump came onto them, liberals believe that, of all people, a washed-up *pornstar* would be most credible and the most feminist! But when it came to Joe Biden's accusers, the least plausible and least feminist was Tara Reade, a former staffer who served under Joe Biden from 1992 until 1993, while he was a US senator. Just a note, Tara Reade has been described as a "liar" and "manipulative" by people who were close with her while others have substantiated her claims. So I can't either give a huge reason to explain why she is or isn't telling the truth when she says Joe Biden raped her.

I wouldn't say Joe Biden is a sexual predator more than he has sexually pervasive tendencies, which could be characterized as creepy. If you ask a Democrat whether or not they are able to list all, if any, of the sexual allegations against Joe Biden, they probably can't. So just for the sake of being informative here's a list of the women who alleged that Joe Biden displayed inappropriate behaviors toward them:

• Lucy Flores: Biden gave her a "big slow kiss" on the back of the head after smelling her hair during a 2014 campaign event;

- Amy Lappos: Lappos is a former congressional aide who alleges that Joe Biden rubbed his nose against hers after pulling her in close to himself during a political fundraiser;
- D. J. Hill: Hill expressed how uncomfortable she felt after a political fundraiser where Joe Biden had placed his hand on her shoulder and began to rub up and down;
- Ally Coll: Biden squeezed her shoulders and complimented her smile for "a beat too long";
- Caitlyn Caruso: After Biden had laid his hand on her for a long period, he laid his hand on her thigh;
- Amy Karasek: Karasek is a sexual assault survivor who had her space violated when Joe Biden grabbed her hands and pressed his forehead against hers;
- Vail Kohnert-Yount: When she was an intern at the White House in 2013, Joe Biden introduced himself by putting

his hand to the back of her head and pressing his forehead against hers; and

- Tara Reade: Reade claims she was fired after "contemplating" going to the authorities to report when Joe Biden had "penetrated" her in 1983 while she was still a staff member under the senator.[114]

At least half of these examples have photographic proof that shows Biden being creepy. So Joe is a creep who doesn't hide the fact he doesn't respect the personal space of women. Maybe Joe thinks *every* woman is his gal.

**Beijing Biden**: It's no secret that Hunter Biden is a no-talent billionaire wannabe. But being a no-talent billionaire wannabe isn't a problem; America happens to be full of them. What *is* a problem is Hunter calling on his pops to help him out. It's a *big* problem because Joe Biden helped his son out while he was still the vice president to Barack Obama.

Joe Biden violated article 1, section 9, clause 8 of the US Constitution, which states, "No title of nobility shall be granted by the United States: and no person holding any office of profit or trust under them, shall, without the consent of the Congress, accept of any present, emolument, office, or title, of any kind whatever, from any king, prince, or foreign State." And in this section, I'll explain why.

If you recall—if you don't, I don't blame you—during the late months of 2013 and early 2014, violent protests broke out in Kyiv, Ukraine, which called for integration into western economies. Zoom forward to April 16, 2014, Vice President Joe Biden met with Devon Archer, his son's business partner. On April 21, five days later, Joe Biden flew to Ukraine on "official business." On April 22, Devon Archer became a part of the board of Burisma.

Coincidentally, six days after Archer joined Burisma, British officials seized $23 million from the private London bank accounts of Mykola Zlochevsky, the Ukrainian owner of Burisma. Fourteen days after that on May 2, Hunter Biden also joined the board of Burisma. It's no hidden secret that over the next few years, Hunter Biden and Devon Archer were paid millions just for being on the board by a corrupt Ukrainian oligarch.

Hunter's position on the board obviously (I think we can all agree) risked being an issue. It could affect America's policies toward Ukraine and vice versa. It definitely affected how Ukrainian politicians treated the Bidens. It wasn't until August 2019 did investigations into the potential conflicts of interest initially begin.

The investigations were launched when the newly administered president pro tempore of the United States Senate Chuck Grassely sent a letter to the Department of Treasury regarding potential conflicts of interest concerning the Obama Administration's policy toward the Henniges transaction. The Henniges transaction was an approved transaction of an American maker of military applicable anti-vibration technology that was given to a Chinese government-owned aviation company and an investment firm "with ties" to the government of China.[115]

I don't know much about anti-whatchamacallits, but the point is that the investigation wasn't initially launched for reasons other than Joe Biden. During Grassley's investigation, it was discovered that during the course of this investigation, the position Hunter Biden had on the board of Burisma was known by the Obama Administration to be problematic and significantly interfered in the handling of Ukraine.

When Victor Shokin, Ukraine's top prosecutor, was invest- igating Burisma's founder and CEO Mykola Zlochevsky, Joe Biden interjected himself into the situation. He threatened to withhold $1 billion worth of United States loan guarantees if Shokin wasn't fired. "I looked at them and said, 'I'm leaving in six hours.'" Joe Biden told a group of people in a leaked video. "If the prosecutor is not fired, you're not getting the money." He went on to say, "Well, son of a bitch. He got fired."[116]

Democrats are probably going to shrug it off and call it a coincidence. But the evidence is too damning to be a simple coincidence. It's not circumstantial, and it's not made up. Joe Biden used his position to help his son out.

Now you know how Joe Biden helped his son out by using his position. But how did he profit from it? Hunter Biden siphoned off millions from lucrative business deals to hand over to his pop, or his "chairman," as he likes to call him. First of all, it's clear from emails that Hunter considered his father to be a business partner along with his uncle because he asked for keys to his office to be made for them.

Second of all, Trump's personal attorney, Rudy Giuliani, released damning text messages from Hunter Biden to his daughter, Naomi, which showed Joe Biden wasn't being given money from his son for his help; he was *taking* money from his son to continue helping him out. "But I don't receive any respect and that's fine I guess."[117] Hunter began. He describes his grueling efforts and tireless labor to support the family. "Works for you, apparently. I hope you all can do what I did and pay for everything for this entire family for 30 years. It's really hard..."[118] Now here's where we see the kind of dad Hunter has, "but don't worry, unlike Pop I won't make you give me half your salary."[119] To be clear, "Pop" is Joe Biden. Hunter doesn't get any respect for being a no-talent, crack-head, sex addict who decided to have a mid-life crisis during his daddy's vice presidency through now.

Third of all, Tony Bobulinski, the whistleblower who wasn't so private, the confidant who wasn't so corrupt; Tony Bobulisnksi is to Joe Biden's Ukrainegate as the tapes were to Nixon's Watergate. In short, Tony Bobulinski can and just might nearly put the entire Biden crime family behind bars for a good while. Tony Bobulinski, a retired lieutenant and the former CEO of SinoHawk, said that the Bidens courted him in an attempt to help him make millions in Hunter's lucrative business. When he confronted Hunter's uncle and Joe's brother, Jim Biden, asking him how they thought they could get away with it, "plausible deniability" was the response he got.[120]

Tony Bobulinski isn't your typical dirty Washington swamp whistleblower. He's not somebody with a political agenda or angle; in fact, he has even donated money to the campaigns of several prominent Democrats in the past. No, he's somebody who put his life and the lives of his entire family on the line to expose Joe Biden for the fraudster he truly is.

He originally wasn't going to blow the whistle on Joe, Bobulinski said.[121] But when Adam Schiff again claimed any accusation against Joe Biden and Hunter was just part of a Russian disinformation campaign, Tony had had it.

It started when a computer repairman received Hunter Biden's own personal laptop. While going through it, the repairman discovered a trove of pornography and very concerning messages. The repairman then uploaded the emails to a couple of USBs and confiscated the laptop to US officials while keeping one USB for himself for safekeeping. When the laptop story broke, it should have shattered any notion that Joe Biden hadn't lied. But the Democrat's mainstream media immediately called it Russian disinformation; I mean, the very few times they briefly covered it.[122]

If you had a Democrat back then about Hunter's laptop, most of them wouldn't have had a clue what you were referring to. Those who did would have had no other knowledge of the laptop except the opinion that it was Russian disinformation. The same thing happened with Tony Bobulinski. The only prominent news channels that broadcast Tony Bobuliski before the presidential debate were *C-SPAN* and *Fox News*.

In fact, the Democrats thought this had been *disproven*. They thought the investigation into Hunter was done and over. But I called it. I *knew* there was and still was an ongoing investigation into Hunter Biden. I said that before Attorney General William Barr confirmed in December 2020 that there had been an investigation since 2019.

Just remember Donald Trump was *impeached* for a perfectly legal phone call with the Ukrainian president, asking him if he had any information to prove Joe Biden was a liar. Turns out, good ol' Don was right. If it was constitutionally plausible, that impeachment label should be undone and reversed.

I do, however, believe Nancy Pelosi can be impeached for misuse or even abuse of power for the multiple times she has interrupted and upset the process of the Constitution; impeached for her continual incitement of left-wing violence, namely when she dismissed the BLM and Antifa rioting, looting, and destruction as "People will do what they do,"[123] impeached for when she withheld the Articles of Impeachment against Donald J. Trump from the Republican-held Senate in December 2019, which infringed on Donald Trump's right to a "fair and speedy trial," and impeached for threatening to impeach Donald Trump if Vice President Mike Pence refused to invoke the 25th

Amendment (another abuse of power). If not impeached, she should have at least been censured. Just wait, Nancy, until the next primary.

So what's the general point of Ukrainegate and Chinagate? If Joe Biden knew about the danger his son was in of losing his position in Burisma, and that's why he had the prosecutor fired, Joe Biden committed a severe crime. And if Joe Biden knowingly mis-prioritized his own personal gain over fulfilling his oath as the vice president, he then committed treason. Finally, Joe Biden used his position as the vice president as leverage in his son's business deals, which resulted in his profiting. He thus ultimately violated the Emoluments Clause (Article 1, Section 9, Article 8 of the Constitution). All of these are impeachable offenses that can be used against now-President Joseph Robinette Biden. Overall, Joe Biden is a sleazeball guy.

# 14.

# THE TRAGIC MISDIRECTION
# OF LIBERALS

I ONCE TOLD A good liberal friend of mine, sometime in October 2020, that "I don't care who runs for governor of California. They can be gay, straight, black, white, Asian, Latino, they can even be transgender, and let me tell you this, I'm okay with that, *as long as* they aren't an activist or Gavin Newsom." Mind you, this was *before* the prospect of a California recall first was disscussed. "Because frankly, what I see in California is a weak-willed man who sits back and lets his state collapse. And I mean this in a serious way, Caitlyn Jenner is more of a man that Newsom. Heck if it was a choice between those two, I'd pick Jenner!"

Now when I said that, I had never heard of a recall or had any possible way of knowing Caitlyn Jenner was thinking of running.

Logically, I would not have imagined that a transgender celebrity, let alone a *Republican* celebrity in California, would run against Newsom in a recall. I'm sure a liberal would never fathom that either. But logic went out the window when Trump won in 2016.

Trump's victory shattered whatever remained of sense and perception of reality the left still had. Liberal culture *is* an agent of destruction. I'm usually not a person to say that ideas are wrong, but I think morals and purposes can be. The most upsetting part of the past forty years is the Democrats' handling of racial justice. Along with their concept of feminism and ethnic-based phobia obsession, the Democrats sure have a misguided sense of equality. It's the tragic misdirection of liberals, baby! So buckle up for perhaps the most confrontational chapter in this book. We're going for a ride!

The worst concept, aside from welfare and fatherless families, that liberals ever conceived was the idea that the only kind of racism is White racism. And I mean this in the most grave sense possible. Liberal Americans have tried to infuse the concept into the minds of American minorities that they are immune from having racially bigoted thoughts.

Liberals will ultimately crush the Black population without laying a finger on them. Seemingly, if you are of any skin color other than white, you're a victim of White privilege. I would say that I really wasn't a benefactor of White privilege. From what I know, my family worked for what they have. I can see there being *rich* privilege, but that only means that the more money you have, the more stuff you can afford. But some wacko will see this and say some stupid nonsense about how my self-conscious and unchecked White privilege blinds me to my harmful and racist rhetoric, which I use to make me feel better for my advantages over minorities, namely Blacks.

I'm truly sick of the crap. Segregation is still around today, but it's not called that. Nowadays, it's called critical race theory. I love diversity; I wish there were more of it where I live. But truthfully, liberals will say one thing but really mean another. When they say racial diversity, what they *really* mean is prevent (conservative) White people from associating with other races. They attacked Amy Coney Barrett because she dared to adopt a Black child. They claimed adopting Black children is today's equivalent of owning slaves. Liberals are becoming more and more intolerant, just like they were not even forty years ago.

Members of the "woke" culture think that because White people had slaves, White people are racist for trying to mingle with Black Americans. Liberals religiously *believe* it's okay to be racially intolerant, only if it's against White people. They are continually telling minorities that it's actually *okay* to be racist. "You're Black," they might say. "You can't truly be racist." Some would say that—just by pointing that out—I'm racist, but I know it's true. I'll give an undeniable example. The remaining World War II veterans who are still alive today—the very same who fought fascism—are being called the worst generation and Nazis. It's sad and upsetting.

Liberals are like chameleons: able to disguise themselves with their surroundings when it benefits them. Most of the outrage you see doesn't come from where you think it would; it comes from White "activists." If you look at footage of rioters in the wake of George Floyd, many of the people who began the trend of looting and destruction were White. A lot of the people pulling down statues were White. White progressive liberal activists aren't there for the meaning of the protest but rather the hype they get from punching people who aren't protesting in the face and the destruction of both public and private property. Each action becomes more extreme and destructive.

It's unfair that most of these rioters, looters, and arsonists get to do what they do—steal, destroy, hurt, and create havoc—get to go home and go to their jobs the next day. It's unfair that Democrats tell the police not to do their jobs (which, ironically, was what they were supposedly protesting) and get away with it. Look at New York City's terrible mayor, Bill De Blasio; he vowed to cut $1 billion out of the NYPD! It's pathetic. It's sad there are a couple of bad cops among the many good. But what I find to be the most unfortunate is the way Democratic politicians pit themselves against the police.

Fake hate crimes are the worst thing to happen in the fight for racial equality. Take Jussie Smollett, for instance. That guy brought shame to the city of Chicago. Apparently, c-class actors like to wear designer sunglasses in the wee small hours of the morning while the whole wide world is fast asleep. Jussie is also prone, on the coldest nights of the year, to get the case of the munchies. Where does one go to satisfy the munchies? No, not your refrigerator, silly! You go to Subway!

Apparently, Chicago is infested with racist, homophobic Trump supporters who crawl out of their hideouts carrying rope and bleach early in the morning, seeking to kill a Black queer actor they probably have never heard of from a show they probably didn't know even existed. And, of course, the most likely period for this to occur would be the single coldest night in Chicago history. I know it's hard to believe, but everything I have just said could actually happen because it's 100 percent factual and consistent on every level, isn't that right, Jussie?[124]

When Jussie "came out," liberals were up in arms, despite the story, which had more holes in it than Bonnie and Clyde's car. Kamala Harris compared the incident to a modern-day lynching. They all agreed this was something Trump would encourage his supporters to do. When some questionable evidence came to light, Kamala did a reverse conga to retract her previous statement. I guess next time, you should wait for the facts to come out. So, Jussie, if you feel bad about what you did, please don't beat yourself up over it.

Professional NASCAR driver Bubba Wallace was threatened with a noose. The noose was hung from his garage door. A White supremacist placed the noose. Bubba was a victim of a hate crime...only...he wasn't. He was the victim of someone tying a standard pull for a garage door, though. But he sure milks it as if he was a victim. He said, "Whether tied in 2019, or whatever, it was a noose."[125] The only thing he indeed can be called a victim of is criticism. It doesn't matter anyway. Bubba got a Root Car Insurance commercial months after the incident, which paints him as a victim of White supremacy, confederates, and Donald John Trump. Sick.

Democrats, like their confederate forebears, continue to use tactics that were designed to protest the United States of America; practices, such as flag burning, segregation, and anti-Republican rhetoric. While Democrats no longer stand for the Confederacy, they sure as hell don't stand for America. They think they stand for "racial justice."

The idea of racial justice isn't sinister or bad, just like treating a person how you would like to be treated. But the Democrat's version of racial justice is an eye for an eye. Someone once said, "An eye for an eye only ends up making the whole world blind." Except, an eye doesn't seem to be good enough. To them, an eye for a head appears more reasonable.

Maybe the best kind of justice is equal justice under the law. That means if a corrupt police officer violates his oath to protect and serve, the courts take care of him. Doesn't that sound better than a cop kills a Black man is equal to burning down countless small family-owned businesses?

The Democrats have a fix-all solution to the question, "What's the answer to how to prevent bad cops?" Why, allowing thugs to loot stores, of course (preferably White-owned)! If a store has nothing good to be stolen, burn it down! Ariel Atkins, a Chicago BLM activist, said looting was the "right" of Black people and "reparations" for slavery.[126]

If looting and arson are forms of reparation, then paid work is slavery. The left doesn't care if it makes sense. In truth, I think they believe the opposite. Anybody with an opinion that resembles reality and logic must be racist.

Less "violent" Democratic politicians think monetary reparations are a better solution. Reparations would have made sense one hundred years ago, not today. A census taken shows that roughly 13 percent of the population is "Black" or "African American."[127] That is approximately around 40 million people. The suggested price given to each African American household is roughly $1 million. It would cost $16 trillion in reparations to achieve that lofty goal. Something that large could only be achieved through taxpayer dollars. The only way to accomplish that would be to increase taxes significantly.

Take Joe Biden, for example; he's playing the game of identity politics. His priority is not to help *all* small businesses harmed during 2020, be it from riots or shut down, but rather minorities first. On January 11, Joe Biden laid out who would be first to receive aid, "Our priority will be Black, Latino, Asian, and Native American owned small businesses, women-owned businesses, and finally having equal access to resources needed to reopen and rebuild."[128]

Joe Biden's campaign promise of "America first" was a lie. It should have been "everybody except for White men first." His slogan, "Build Back Better" should have been "Build Back Bigotry."

On January 6, 2021, a mob of Trump supporters stormed Capitol Hill. They were protesting the election results. Personally, it was a massive disappointment for me. The people who broke in were no better than Antifa and BLM activists who rioted earlier in 2020. I condemned, earlier in the book, *all* types of violent groups. But for Republicans to disrupt the constitutional process in such a matter is disgusting. Republicans are better than what America saw that day.

Of course, there were Antifa actors instigating them to break through the barrier and into the chambers of Capitol Hill. Have you ever seen a Trump supporter go to a rally or protest wearing tactical gear and black helmets carrying ropes and hammers? I don't think so. The Democrats as a whole pointed the finger at Trump. They evidently forgot that when you point a finger at someone, three point back. Twitter and Facebook banned him from his Twitter acccount indefinitely.[129]

For the entirety of four years, Republicans faced false accusations, investigations, and degradations from Democrats. People can only stand a four-year Russian hoax, labeled fascists, Antifa attacks, Democrats allowing violent activists to destroy American businesses, and cancel culture for so long before they snap.

Where were the Democrats when American cities were being overrun for months on end? Where were the politicians when hardworking Americans were losing the livelihoods—that they had been working their entire lives for—overnight? Where were the politicians when activists burned down police stations? Where were liberal politicians when activists tried to flood Trump's RNC speech and beat up as many people as possible?

Republicans asked for a fair election in 2020, and they were shut up. But when the Democrats asked for a fair election in 2016, they got a four-year investigation into conspiracy theory—which in 2020, was discovered to be a scheme stirred up by the Clinton campaign—and they still aren't satisfied. I know I'm not the only one who sees the level of hypocrisy here.

Trump didn't fuel the fire; the Democrats did. Trump was the one who understood Republicans, listened to them, and stood up for them. Democrats did not. Democrats vilified, discredited, canceled, dehumanized, and attacked Republicans for years to a level that has never been seen before. Americans have had their freedoms infringed, their rights taken away, their beliefs assaulted, and all for what? For Trump? No, for America.

The Democratic Party would have you believe that one man—evidently, Trump—could've destroyed all of America. Trump wouldn't have been the one to destroy America; anti-American rhetoric would. It's doing it now. If either party would just listen to the other, America would be a better country.

Another tragic misdirection of the liberal party is feminism. I'll be as blunt as Emily Blunt is. How is infanticide feminism? The argument is that a woman's body means that she gets to decide whether a human being lives or dies. If someone tells her it's immoral, they must be sexist. I just don't get the logic.

My argument is since giving life is one of the most sacred jobs a woman can do, then why are liberals *encouraging* women to get abortions? For radical feminists, being the one to be able to take away life is more empowering than giving it. To them, abortion doesn't prevent the miracle of life from happening, it prevents a baby from happening. Abortion actually prevents miracles from happening.

When a woman "accidentally" gets pregnant, I and many others believe it's then the responsibility of that person to take care of the baby. But liberals think mistakes can be erased. Abortion is a solution, not a consequence. If every mistake could be erased, nobody would learn anything. Pregnancy is a life lesson; it shouldn't be an option just to end one. But if Democrats ever get their way, abortion would be about as accessible as a mobile phone, as usual as a bank loan, and treated as an everyday occurrence.

I think abortion is both a legal and moral issue. If you get yourself pregnant, deal with the consequences. If you had the choice to have sex and get pregnant, you lose the option to stop the pregnancy. If you were irresponsible and didn't use proper protection, don't punish an unborn child. Democrats are seriously thinking about state-funded abortions. It's sickening. It's like how Russia pays parents to hand their children over to the government.

Real feminism is the belief in the equality of sexes that both genders contribute an equal amount. The feminism the Democrats promote is a terrifying kind. Their version of feminism is revenge against men. It is payback for the old concept of the quiet, obedient, cook-and-clean housewife. Apparently, masculinity is toxic. What is their version of masculinity? Is it the stereotypical husband-who-goes-to-work-while-the-wife-stays-home masculinity? They believe men are prone to thinking women are incapable of doing the kind of work men do, and that's just not true!

The kind of women that liberals think are feminists is just shameful. They believe that prostitutes, strippers, and women who get abortions for irresponsible pregnancies display exceptional femininity. They believe that a woman who says men suck is brilliant. No one gives me credit when I speak what everyone is thinking—that sauerkraut sucks.

A real feminist is a person who shows that she can live and work side-by-side with men as an equal. Women who I think embody true feminism are Lucille Ball, Harriett Tubman, Mary Shelly, Justice Amy Coney Barrett, Nancy Reagan, Susan B. Anthony, Mary Tylor Moore, Judy Garland, Queen Victoria, Sally Ride, Christa McAuliffe, Ruth Bader Ginsburg, and Ella Fitzgerald. These are the people who paved the way for equality, not Michelle Obama, Taylor Swift, Cardi B, Ilhan Omar, or Hillary Clinton. Those are just actors who wear feminism as a badge to promote their careers. But the badges they show off are about as meaningful as a cheap plastic minor-league baseball participation award trophy that was made in China that you bought as a part of a twelve-pack you ordered from Oriental Trading for $9.99. In short, it is meaningless.

At the end of a recent Congressional prayer, Congress*man* E*man*ual Cleaver ended his prayer with *amen* followed by an *awomen*. His woke prayer sparked sharp criticism from *man*y people. He called it a "joke."[130]

Since toxic masculinity now comes in the form of words, here is a list of words that need to be changed or modified immediately!

A*men*: Awomen, *Mail* Man: Femail Woman, *Mal[e]*practice: Femalpractice, Hu*man*: Huwoman, *Man*ager: Womanager, *Man*ifestation: Womanifestation, Ro*man*: Rowoman, *Man*ipulation: Womanipulation, *Man*ufacture: Womanufacture, *Male*volence, Femalevolence, *Man*atee, Womanatee, Sports*man*ship: Sportswoman-ship, *Man*ners: Womanners, Crafts*man*ship: Craftswomanship, Ro*man*ce: Rowomance, De*man*ding: Dewomanding, Ger*man*: Gerwoman, Com*man*der: Comwomander, Repri*man*d: Repriwomand, and so on...

You get the idea.

Radical liberals and Democrats achieve their agendas—which they claim to be full of racial equality policies—through morally defunct measures. Attacking Christian beliefs is a go-to favorite of theirs. But that's only one of the five attack targets liberals focus on. If you are all five, you're the worst. Here is a checklist of qualities that the "woke" culture dislikes:

❑ Are you White/Caucasian (or just didn't vote for Joe Biden);

❑ Are you Republican;

❑ Are you straight/heterosexual;

❑ Are you a man/guy/male/dude and prefer your pronouns as he/him and have XY chromosomes to match; and

❑ Are you Christian (or have a general belief in God)?

If you are one of the unfortunate souls who happens to check all five boxes, may God—who is undoubtedly a vegan Democratic- Socialist, and who may or may not be (but likely is) a woman or a nonbinary being who is a yoga instructor on Saturdays and Tuesdays from 10 a.m. to 1:30 p.m.—have mercy on your soul. Amen and Awomen.

There are plenty of articles printed in magazine columns and news-papers talking about how White Christians suck. One article posted by *Religion Dispatches* written by Daniel Shultz titled "The Left Behind: Why Are White American Christians so Racist?" claims that White Christians are literally irredeemably racist.[131] Shultz thinks that "the truth is that white American Christians suck at racial equality."[132] He goes on to say that Whites are unable to see how they contribute and benefit from racial injustice. Hold on; it gets worse. Later in the article, he asks a disgustingly black and white question, "So can white Christian America be saved?"[133] Besides being a question I'm sure nobody rea-sonable, Black or White, has ever asked themselves, his answer is even more disgusting: "Why do you want to save it?"[134]

Liberals have so-called "studies" in which they dissect racism. The studies are, more or less, just rooms full of like-minded liberal students and professors who, day after day, fabricate made-up breakthroughs. The truth is the belief that the root of all racism comes from White Christians. They never stop and think, "Maybe Democrats are culpable?"

Their "diverse" thinking is just something they say to explain why they always take an opposite stance than conservatives.

Whenever a conservative (or anybody other than a woke liberal) voices a reasonably modest opinion about racism, religion, or politics, they are besmirched and belittled. Muslims can't be sexist, Hispanics can't be racist, African-Americans can't be Republicans; these are all stereotypes Democrats have for minorities in the US. Zouhair Mazouz knows that it's the God honest truth. Mazouz is a former Muslim who fled the Islamic religion in 2013 and came to the United States. In an article titled, "Getting It Wrong About Islam: Check Your Secular Privilege, Liberal America," Mazouz expresses how he was ostracized for being "Islamophobic" just for "criticizing the misogynistic treatment of women in predominantly Muslim societies."[135] That's how it goes; you're a victim until you address the severe issues in the Middle East.

The Democrats have continued a series of an unending hail of attacks that could be described as a war on Trump. It wasn't a war to stop him from moving into the White House; it wasn't a war to stop him from winning a second term. It was and is a war to stop us, conservatives, as a whole, from being a part of American life by continually berating, ignoring, and canceling us. The battles were begun by elitist snobs who valued Liberalism over individualism. They often like to say that their common shared interest between their base and conservatives is unity, but I haven't seen much willingness from them to defend and protect the rights of those whom they disagree with since 2015.

In 2016, the Democrats were all set for a typical election cycle. With Hillary Clinton as their predictable figurehead, it was almost certain that the election was theirs. Yeah, Donald Trump was in the race, but who would vote for a guy who was running on the Republican ticket after being a lifelong Democrat, not to mention being a New

York Playboy billionaire businessman? Why worry? At the time, it may not have seemed as if the Trump train would have enough fuel to make it very far. Democrats didn't take him or his base seriously, and they paid for it. To them, Trump was just promoting his brand by thrusting himself in front of the American people—and liberals were more than happy to hand him the megaphone.

Late-night shows booked him; their writers loved the guy. Even SNL (Sad Not Laughable) had him host their show! *CNN* ran an opinion piece in July 2015, praising him as "God's Gift to Comedy".[136] The writer of that article, Jon Macks, showered Trump with his love and concluded his piece with a personal message to Donald: "So Mr. Trump, please know that I am one Democrat who supports your candidacy, and I urge you to stay the course. And in the event the money starts to dry up, please know I am prepared, as I suspect all late-night writers are, to write a check to keep you going."[137]

In February the following year, *CNN* became a bit worried about "God's Gift." How was it that Trump was still here? Why hadn't he dropped out yet? Was he seriously thinking of becoming president when he announced his candidacy? *CNN* changed their tune in an opinion piece titled, "Donald Trump can win—and he must be stopped," stating that "he ought to have crashed and burned as a Republican presidential candidate weeks ago."[138] After seeing the stark contrast, it's no wonder Dems were so surprised when he beat Hillary Clinton; they thought he was a joke for most of his presidential campaign! Hillary was their Alec Baldwin of politicians, but then along came Trump, who turned out to be the Matthew McConaughey of politicians, and completely creamed the competition.

If I remember correctly—but correct me if I'm wrong—Joe Biden promised, ***promised*** unity; he said he would work with Democrats and Republicans to get things done. Yet since he said those words on inauguration day, he has done nothing to show for that promise—just more empty words from a lifetime politician from the Washington establishment. Let's recap some things from his first forty-five days in office, shall we?

- On his very first day, he signed fifteen executive orders, the majority of which repealed Trump's executive orders;
- He didn't express that the impeachment divided political parties since the majority of conservatives opposed it;
- He called people in Texas who were dying to take off their masks and reopen their state as "neanderthal," despite the fact that he waited until after the deep freeze ended to hand these cavemen blankets. I guess he wanted to see if these Neanderthals were capable of making fire before weighing in;
- His claims that the Trump administration left the vaccine rollout plan in tatters—obviously forgetting that were it not for Operation Warp Speed, the entire world would still be without a single vaccine; and
- His handling of the border crisis, yes crisis. He promised to give amnesty to the hundreds of thousands of unaccompanied migrant minors (under eighteen). Wait—what happened to the parents of these migrant children that Trump was supposedly separating? And then he lied about the amount of how many immigrants were being turned away; the truth of which was that migrant facilities were more cramped and left absolutely no room for social distancing.

Joe Biden is more like Shooting Bull Biden.

Do I need to even to mention his failure in Afghanistan which resulted in the rise of ISIS-K, the tragic murder of 13 service men, and the abandonment of hundreds of American citizens? Joe Biden has worse foreign policies than Jimmy Carter, and that's a high bar to reach.

The issue with the Democratic Party today is that it weighs equity over equality, vigilantism over the justice system, teacher unions over students, politically correct speech over free speech, collectivism over individualism, socialism over capitalism, and violent rioters over police (except for when it makes Republicans look bad). Unity really isn't how they plan on getting anything achieved. So before the next mid-terms, when it comes to getting as much done as they can, Democrat lawmakers will be like Vegas tourists: fast and loose.

The Democratic Party *was* directly responsible for many of the atrocities committed ages ago in America, but I'm not saying they need to beg for forgiveness, yet they do that all by themselves. Their solution to racism, sexism, and other types of "isms" is to overcorrect. It's like a dentist; if you have an overbite that needs to be fixed, they fix it. But if they overcorrect that overbite, you're stuck with an underbite and go on looking like Popeye the Sailor for the rest of your life.

So when the Democrats began overcorrecting, they made everything too complicated to straighten out. They made everyone a victim who was not a White straight man. You are a victim of toxic masculinity until you say modern feminism is going overboard. You are a victim of racism unless you're a conservative. It's victim, victim, victim, until, until, until—a never-ending cycle of identity politics.

# 15.

# AND NOW, THE END IS (HERE)

WHELP, IT SEEMS THAT you were able to reach the end of my little book, finally; it took you long enough. But I genuinely hope you have thoroughly enjoyed reading it. My only wish is that you took something away from it. Either I impressed upon you some very thought-provoking concepts, or I just ended up traumatizing you for life (I seriously doubt I made that much of a lasting impact).

I placed my heart into this book in an attempt to make a connection with you, the "people." Throughout our journey, we laughed, and we cried. So while I ranted, I'm hoping I was able to open your eyes. It's unfortunate our time together was so brief, but it's a book; what did you expect?

I just want you to remember a few things. The first is that no matter if you are a Democrat or a Republican, religious or not, Black or White, straight or gay, born in America or not—if you believe that America gets better because of the exercise of the fundamental rights given to us over two centuries ago, you're a true American. You don't have to give an arm and a leg to be a patriot. All you need to do is stand up for others. Remember, there is always someone weaker than you, someone who needs somebody like *you* to stand up for their constitutional rights, and always somebody who believes in you. *I* believe in you.

My second point is America's under attack. It's being assailed by political correctness, cancel culture, woke liberals, corrupt career politicians, liars, phony investigations that go nowhere, liberal social media platforms, and vindicative Democrats who want to tear you down. Don't let them do it to you. You have the power to fight systematic suppression and oppression. Never stop fighting injustice. Fight like hell! Figuratively, of course.

My third point is the most simple of all. Our country is rapidly changing; that's indisputable. But how is it changing? Do you see a positive change or negative one? If we, collectively as Americans, don't see the direction we're headed in and unilaterally identify the problem, I can tell you that it won't be pretty. Here's the surefire way to embody the American spirit. If you're being silenced for being unlike everyone else, speak up louder. If you feel misrepresented, be proactive and represent what you want people to see. When you're unhappy with the current state of things, you still have your First Amendment rights. If anyone tells you otherwise, they're lying.

And finally, remember, freedom isn't free. It's not that you have to start an uprising to keep it; you just have to remember you have it and why you have it.

As I said at the beginning of this book, you can take one absolute truth away from being an American. The basic principles of your constitutional rights to "life, liberty, and the pursuit of happiness" are written down as our inalienable rights and are the truest words ever to form a nation.

The left will deceive you, seduce you, and manipulate you to get you to accept and accommodate to their kind of world. They will stop at nothing to make you believe that you're a victim of America. You're only a victim if you want to be. Once you allow yourself to believe you're weak, you start to self-victimize. But if you believe you have the ability to overcome, you will.

Don't become a fly caught in a web; because that's what the false narrative is. False narratives like Antifa aren't real—America is systemically racist, conservatives hate minorities, and cops are fascists—are part of an intricate deception. Those who believe in America know the truth. The truth is that the power-hungry have created a web of lies, one in which you're supposed to believe that America is founded on hate.

Those who oppose their warped system will continue to fight. Those who fall into the roles they are given will continue to fail. It's as simple as that. Who are *you* going to be? Which narrative are you going to believe? *I* choose to believe in America.

# ENDNOTES

1   Jill Lapore. "How the Simulmatics Corporation
Invented the Future." The New Yorker. July 27, 2020.
https://www.newyorker.com/magazine/2020/08/03/
how-the-simulmatics-corporation-invented-the-future

2   Wikipedia. "1960 United States presidential election",
Wikipedia, September 29, 2020, https://en.wikipedia.org/
wiki/1960_United_States_presidential_election

3   Eileen McNamara. "Enough With The Kennedy Dynasty Hot
Takes. Joe Lost Because He Was Impatient". WBUR. September
02, 2020, https://www.wbur.org/cognoscenti/2020/09/02/
joe-kennedy-ed-markey-senate-race-eileen-mcnamara

4   National Park Services. "Theodore Roosevelt and Conservation."
National Park Services. November 16, 2017. https://www.nps.
gov/thro/learn/historyculture/theodore-roosevelt-and-conser-
vation.htm

5   U.S. Federal Highway Administration. "Why President
Dwight D. Eisenhower Understood We Needed the Interstate
System," U.S. Department of Transportation/Federal Highway
Administration, July 24, 2017, https://www.fhwa.dot.gov/inter-
state/brainiacs/eisenhowerinterstate.cfm

6   Wikipedia. "Tear Down This Wall". Wikipedia. October 7, 2020.
https://en.wikipedia.org/wiki/Tear_down_this_wall!#:~:tex-
t=%22Tear%20down%20this%20wall%22%2C,Berlin%20on%20

June%2012%2C%201987.&text=Though%20it%20received%20
relatively%20little,fall%20of%20the%20Berlin%20Wall.

7   Donald J. Trump for President, Inc., "Timeline of
    Accomplishments," Promises Kept, August 31,2020. https://www.
    promiseskept.com/timeline/

8   Democratic National Committee. "Our History". Democratic
    National Committee, 2020, https://democrats.org/who-we-are/
    our-history/

9   Will Englund. "Russia's orphans: Government takes cus-
    tody of children when parents can't cope" The Washington
    Post. May 04, 2013. https://www.washingtonpost.com/world/
    russias-orphans-government-takes-custody-of-children-
    when-parents-cant-cope/2013/05/02/4d17ff4a-a757-11e2-a8e2-
    5b98cb59187f_story.html

10  Emily Venezky. "Donald Trump doesn't meet the defini-
    tion of morbidly obese". Politifact. May 19, 2020. https://
    www.politifact.com/factchecks/2020/may/19/nancy-pelosi/
    no-he-not-morbidly-obese/

11  Emily Venezky. "Donald Trump doesn't meet the defini-
    tion of morbidly obese". Politifact. May 19, 2020. https://
    www.politifact.com/factchecks/2020/may/19/nancy-pelosi/
    no-he-not-morbidly-obese/

12  Emily Venezky. "Donald Trump doesn't meet the defini-
    tion of morbidly obese". Politifact. May 19, 2020. https://
    www.politifact.com/factchecks/2020/may/19/nancy-pelosi/
    no-he-not-morbidly-obese/

13  Mark J. Kohler. "How Joe Biden's Tax Plan Could Affect Small-
    Business Owners," Entrepreneur. September 29, 2020. https://
    www.entrepreneur.com/article/356890 (video)

14  Samantha Putterman. "Fact-checking claims
    that Biden called troops 'stupid bastards' in resur-
    faced video," Politico. Sept 28, 2020. https://www.

politifact.com/factchecks/2020/sep/28/instagram-posts/
fact-checking-claims-biden-called-troops-stupid-ba/

15  Andrew Duehren and James T. Areddy, "Hunter Biden's
Ex-Business Partner Alleges Father Knew About Venture," The
Wall Street Journal. October 23, 2020, https://www.wsj.com/
articles/hunter-bidens-ex-business-partner-alleges-father-knew-
about-venture-11603421247

16  Caleb Parke. "Sen. Cotton calls out Obama-Biden admin,
Clinton on Russia collusion hoax". Fox News. October 7, 2020.
https://www.foxnews.com/politics/biden-clinton-obama-trump-
russia-collusion-hoax-sen-tom-cotton

17  Eugene Kiely. "The FBI Files on Clinton's Emails," FactCheck.
org. September 7, 2016. https://www.factcheck.org/2016/09/
the-fbi-files-on-clintons-emails/

18  Fox News. "FBI discussed interviewing Michael Flynn 'to get
him to lie' and 'get him fired,' handwritten notes show". Fox
News. April 30, 2020. https://www.foxnews.com/politics/
michael-flynn-fbi-handwritten-notes-get-him-lie-fired

19  The Editorial Board, "All the Adam Schiff Transcripts" The Wall
Street Journal, May 12, 2020. https://www.wsj.com/articles/
all-the-adam-schiff-transcripts-11589326164

20  NBC News. "Trump slams Biden's record: 'I ran because of you',"
NBC News, October 22, 2020. https://www.nbcnews.com/video/
trump-slams-biden-s-record-i-ran-because-of-you-94449221652

21  Emily Ekins, "The State of Free Speech and Tolerance in
America", Cato Institute, October 31, 2017. https://www.cato.
org/survey-reports/state-free-speech-tolerance-america

22  Geoffrey Skelley and Anna Wiederkehr, "Trump Is Losing
Ground With White Voters But Gaining Among Black And
Hispanic Americans" ThirtyFiveEight, October 19, 2020. https://
fivethirtyeight.com/features/trump-is-losing-ground-with-
white-voters-but-gaining-among-black-and-hispanic-americans/

23  Paul Steinhauser, "Biden says 'you ain't black' if torn between him and Trump, in dustup with Charlamagne tha God," Fox News, May 22, 2020. https://www.foxnews.com/politics/biden-torn-him-and-trump-aint-black-in-dust-up-with-charlamagne-tha-god

24  Joseph Wulfsohn, "Biden again praises Latino diversity as being 'unlike the African American community'," Fox News, August 6, 2020. https://www.foxnews.com/politics/biden-latino-diversity-african-american-community

25  Casey Tolan, "Campaign fact check: Here's how Kamala Harris really prosecuted marijuana cases", Mercury News, September 11, 2019. https://www.mercurynews.com/2019/09/11/kamala-harris-prosecuting-marijuana-cases/

26  Tyler Olsen, "Bail fund backed by Kamala Harris and Joe Biden staffers bailed out alleged child abuser, docs indicate", Fox News, September 17, 2020, https://www.foxnews.com/politics/bail-fund-backed-by-kamala-harris-and-biden-staffers-bailed-out-alleged-child-abuser

27  Jeff Charles, "Media Takes an Interesting Lesson from Karl Marx", Liberty Nation New, August 20, 2018. https://www.libertynation.com/media-takes-a-lesson-from-karl-marx/

28  Evan Bush, "Welcome to the Capitol Hill Autonomous Zone, where Seatlle Protestors Gather without Police", The SeattleTimes, August 12, 2020. https://www.seattletimes.com/seattle-news/welcome-to-the-capitol-hill-autonomous-zone-where-seattle-protesters-gather-without-police/

29  Marx21. "About", Marx21 US. October 30, 2020(date accessed). https://marx21us.org/about/

30  Just Jared, "Bernie Sanders Celeb Supporters: 35 Stars Who Endorsed Him!", Just Jared. February 25, 2020, http://www.justjared.com/2020/02/25/bernie-sanders-celeb-supporters-35-stars-who-endorsed-him/

31  Brittany Bernstein. "Biden Says Antifa Is 'An Idea, Not An Organization' during Presidential Debate," National Review, September 29, 2020. https://www.nationalreview.com/news/biden-says-antifa-is-an-idea-not-an-organization-during-presidential-debate/

32  Kyle Shildeler, "The Real History of Antifa," American Mind, June 3, 2020, https://americanmind.org/essays/the-real-history-of-antifa/

33  Paul Goldberg, "Jesse Watters Interviews Portland Mayor Candidate Who Tweeted 'I am Antifa'" News Thud, September 7, 2020, https://newsthud.com/jesse-watters-interviews-portland-mayor-candidate-who-tweeted-i-am-antifa/

34  The Editors of the Encyclopedia Brittanica, "Black Lives Matter", Brittanica, Date Accessed: August 2, 2021. https://www.britannica.com/topic/social-movement

35  Chicago Tribune Staff, "George Floyd fallout: Here's what happened May 31 in the Chicago area" Chicago Tribune, May 31, 2020, https://www.chicagotribune.com/news/breaking/ct-george-floyd-chicago-protests-20200531-qghf4l7ysjgl3etxqu-3jv6oq6a-story.html

36  Ashley Cole, "David Dorn's widow speaks at Republican National Convention," 5 on Your Side, August 28, 2020. https://www.ksdk.com/article/news/politics/ann-dorn-republican-national-convention/63-51301c9d-6b85-414f-a2c2-58f807d9856f

37  Ian Schwartz, "Seattle Mayor Durkan: CHAZ Has A 'Block Party Atmosphere' Could Turn Into 'Summer Of Love'", Real Clear Politics, June 12, 2020. https://www.realclearpolitics.com/video/2020/06/12/seattle_mayor_durkan_chaz_has_a_block_party_atmosphere_could_turn_into_summer_of_love.html

38  Gallup/Knight Foundation Survey, "Perceived Accuracy and Bias in the News Media" Knight Foundation, March 11, 2018, https://knightfoundation.org/wp-content/uploads/2020/03/KnightFoundation_AccuracyandBias_Report_FINAL.pdf

39  Gallup/Knight Foundation Survey, "Perceived Accuracy and Bias in the News Media" Knight Foundation, March 11, 2018, https://knightfoundation.org/wp-content/uploads/2020/03/KnightFoundation_AccuracyandBias_Report_FINAL.pdf

40  Brian Flood, "Stephen Colbert, Jimmy Fallon roast Trump with 97% of political jokes over Biden, study says", Fox News, October 20, 2020. https://www.foxnews.com/entertainment/stephen-colbert-jimmy-fallon-mock-trump-97-percent-political-jokes-over-biden-study-says

41  Marisa Schultz & Brooke Singman, "Twitter locks official Trump campaign account over sharing Hunter Biden video," Fox News. October 19, 2020. https://www.foxnews.com/politics/twitter-trump-campaign-account-video-hunter-biden

42  Joseph A. Wulfsohn, "Twitter censors Trump's tweet knocking Supreme Court's Pa. vote, Facebook also cracks down," Fox News, November 2, 2020. https://www.foxnews.com/media/twitter-censors-trumps-tweet-knocking-supreme-courts-pa-vote-facebook-also-cracks-down

43  Brian Flood, "Twitter, Facebook have censored Trump 65 times compared to zero for Biden, study says" Fox News, October 19, 2020. https://www.foxnews.com/media/twitter-facebook-have-censored-trump-65-times-compared-to-zero-for-biden-study-says

44  Brian Flood, "Twitter briefly suspends CBP Commissioner Mark Morgan after he touts success of border wall," Fox News, October 29, 2020. https://www.foxnews.com/media/twitter-suspends-mark-morgan-praising-border-wall

45  Joseph Wulfsohn, "Twitter censors Trump's Minneapolis tweet for 'glorifying violence'," Fox News, May 29, 2020. https://www.foxnews.com/politics/twitter-cracks-down-on-trumps-minneapolis-tweet-says-it-glorifies-violence

46  Adam Shaw, Trump campaign press secretary temporarily suspended on Twitter over mail-in voting tweet," Fox

News. October 22, 2020. https://www.foxnews.com/politics/
trump-press-secretary-suspended-twitter

47  Joseph Wulfson, "Twitter locks out Kayleigh McEnany from
her personal account for sharing New York Post's Hunter Biden
report," Fox News, October 14, 2020. https://www.foxnews.com/
media/twitter-locks-out-kayleigh-mcenany-hunter-biden

48  Gregg Re, "Twitter exec in charge of effort to fact-check Trump
has history of anti-Trump posts, called McConnell a 'bag of
farts,'" Fox News, May 27, 2020, https://www.foxnews.com/pol-
itics/twitter-exec-in-charge-of-effort-to-fact-check-trump-has-
history-of-anti-trump-posts-called-mcconnell-a-bag-of-farts

49  Marisa Schultz, "Twitter dings Trump tweet on voting in
North Carolina: 'Voting twice in North Carolina is illegal,'" Fox
News, September 12, 2020. https://www.foxnews.com/politics/
twitter-trump-tweet-voting-north-carolina-voting-illegal

50  Gregg Re, "Twitter locks out McConnell's campaign for posting
video of calls for violence at his home," Fox News, August 8,
2019, https://www.foxnews.com/politics/twitter-locks-out-mcco-
nnell-campaign-for-posting-video-of-calls-for-violence-at-mc-
connells-home

51  Edmund DeMarche, "Twitter deletes video promoted by Trump
on hydroxychloroquine use for coronavirus," Fox News, July
28, 2020. https://www.foxnews.com/politics/twitter-post-that-
seems-to-show-doctors-praising-hydroxychloroquine-use-for-
coronavirus

52  James Rogers, "Twitter slammed for 'shadow banning' prominent Republicans" Fox News, July
25, 2018. "https://www.foxnews.com/tech/
twitter-slammed-for-shadow-banning-prominent-republicans"

53  Marcy Gordon, "Facebook, Twitter CEOs facing questions on
election measures," Fox61, November 17, 2020. https://www.
fox61.com/article/news/nation-world/facebook-twitter-ceos-fac-
ing-questions-on-election-measures/507-114b3929-b040-45b0-
a0a4-67309b628dc4

54 Todd Spangler, "Twitter Unblocks Account of New York Post, Which Claims Victory in Standoff Over Biden Stories," Variety, October 31, 2020. https://variety.com/2020/digital/news/twitter-unblocks-new-york-post-hunter-biden-hacked-materials-1234820449/

55 Rachel Elbaum, "Johnny Depp Raises 'Last Time an Actor Assassinated a President'", NBC News, June 23, 2020. https://www.nbcnews.com/pop-culture/pop-culture-news/johnny-depp-when-was-last-time-actor-assassinated-president-n775881

56 "Madonna, at Women's March on Washington, says she has thought about 'blowing up the White House'" CBS News, January 21, 2020. https://www.cbsnews.com/news/madonna-womens-march-washington-dc-white-house/

57 Path2USA, "US Citizenship - 10 Necessary Steps to Become a US Citizen," Path2USA, Date obtained: June 10, 2021, https://www.path2usa.com/us-citizenship-steps

58 Abby Budiman, "Key Findings About U.S. Immigrants," Pew Research Center, August 20, 2020, https://www.pewresearch.org/fact-tank/2020/08/20/key-findings-about-u-s-immigrants/

59 Abby Budiman, "Key Findings About U.S. Immigrants," Pew Research Center, August 20, 2020, https://www.pewresearch.org/fact-tank/2020/08/20/key-findings-about-u-s-immigrants/

60 Laura Widener, "US-Mexico border deaths lower per year under Trump than Obama, data shows," American Military News, June 27, 2019. https://americanmilitarynews.com/2019/06/us-mexico-border-deaths-lower-under-trump-than-obama-data-shows/

61 Jasper Gilardi,"Ally or Exploiter? The Smuggler-Migrant Relationship is a Complex One" Migration Policy Institute, February 5, 2020, https://www.migrationpolicy.org/article/ally-or-exploiter-smuggler-migrant-relationship-complex-one

62  Executive Order 9066, February 19, 1942; General Records of the United States Government; Record Group 11; National Archives.

63  Bilal Qureshi, "From Wrong To Right: A U.S. Apology For Japanese Internment" NPR, August 9, 2013. https://www.npr.org/sections/codeswitch/2013/08/09/210138278/japanese-internment-redress

64  Miriam Valverde, "Fact-checking Biden on use of cages for immigrants during Obama administration" Politifact, September 13, 2020. https://www.politifact.com/factchecks/2019/sep/13/joe-biden/fact-checking-biden-use-cages-during-obama-adminis/

65  The Wall Street Journal, "HBO Max Pulls 'Gone With the Wind' While "Cops" Get Canceled," Fox Business, June 10, 2020, https://www.foxbusiness.com/lifestyle/hbo-max-gone-with-the-wind-cops-canceled

66  The Academy of Motion Picture Arts and Sciences, "Academy Establishes Representation and Inclusion Standards for OSCARs® Eligibility." Oscars, September 8, 2020. https://www.oscars.org/news/academy-establishes-representation-and-inclusion-standards-oscarsr-eligibility

67  The Academy of Motion Picture Arts and Sciences, "Academy Establishes Representation and Inclusion Standards for OSCARs® Eligibility." Oscars, September 8, 2020. https://www.oscars.org/news/academy-establishes-representation-and-inclusion-standards-oscarsr-eligibility

68  The Academy of Motion Picture Arts and Sciences, "Academy Establishes Representation and Inclusion Standards for OSCARs® Eligibility." Oscars, September 8, 2020. https://www.oscars.org/news/academy-establishes-representation-and-inclusion-standards-oscarsr-eligibility

69  Esther O'Reilly, "Cancelled To Death: The Mike Adams I Knew," The American Conservative, July 30, 2020.

https://www.theamericanconservative.com/articles/
cancelled-to-death-the-mike-adams-i-knew/

70    Stephanie K. Baer, "A Professor who was Known for his Racist,
      Misogynistic Tweets was Found Dead in his Home," BuzzFeed
      News, July 23, 2020. https://www.buzzfeednews.com/article/
      skbaer/mike-adams-uncw-professor-death

71    David K. Li, "Professor Behind 'vile' racist and sexist tweets
      found dead in North Carolina home," NBC News, July 24, 2020.
      https://www.nbcnews.com/news/us-news/professor-behind-vile-
      racist-sexist-tweets-found-dead-north-carolina-n1234801

72    Ryan Lizza, Daniel Lippman, Meredith McGraw," AOC wants
      to cancel those who worked for Trump. Good luck with that,
      they say" Politico, September 9, 2020, https://www.politico.com/
      news/2020/11/09/aoc-cancel-worked-for-trump-435293

73    Ryan Lizza, Daniel Lippman, Meredith McGraw," AOC wants
      to cancel those who worked for Trump. Good luck with that,
      they say" Politico, September 9, 2020, https://www.politico.com/
      news/2020/11/09/aoc-cancel-worked-for-trump-435293

74    Bobby Burack, "Kieth Olbermann is the Worst,"
      OutKick, November 2020, https://www.outkick.com/
      keith-olbermann-is-the-worst/

75    Bobby Burack, "Kieth Olbermann is the Worst,"
      OutKick, November 2020, https://www.outkick.com/
      keith-olbermann-is-the-worst/

76    The British Library Board, "Learning Voices of the Holocaust:
      Anti-Jewish Decrees" British Library, June 11, 2006, https://www.
      bl.uk/learning/histcitizen/voices/info/decrees/decrees.html

77    Jennifer Raff, "What Do Elizabeth Warren's DNA Test Results
      Actually Mean?" Forbes, October 15, 2018, https://www.forbes.
      com/sites/jenniferraff/2018/10/15/what-do-elizabeth-warrens-
      dna-test-results-actually-mean/?sh=429a777112df

[78] Ellen Cranely, "Ilhan Omar responded to the son of a 9/11 victim who criticized her in his speech at ground zero", Business Insider, September 15, 2019, https://www.businessinsider.com/ilhan-omar-september-11-comments-2019-9

[79] Cody Nelson, "Minnesota Congresswoman Ignites Debate On Israel And Anti-Semitism," NPR, March 7, 2020, https://www.npr.org/2019/03/07/700901834/minnesota-congresswoman-ignites-debate-on-israel-and-anti-semitism

[80] Bruce Haring, "'Face The Nation' Confronts Rep. Ilhan Omar On Her 9/11 Comments – She Focuses On Muslim Backlash", Deadline, September 15, 2019, https://deadline.com/2019/09/face-the-nation-confronts-rep-ilhan-omar-on-her-9-11-comments-1202735153/

[81] Dan Clark, "Trump's tax plan is "completely focused on the wealthy and the powerful - not the middle class" Politifact, October 8, 2017, https://www.politifact.com/factchecks/2017/oct/09/charles-schumer/does-trumps-tax-plan-do-nothing-low-income-earners/

[82] Molly Hensley-Clancy, "Stafers, Documents Show Amy Klobuchar's Wrath Toward Her Aides," BuzzFeed News, February 8, 2019, https://www.buzzfeednews.com/article/mollyhensleyclancy/amy-klobuchar-staff-2020-election

[83] Molly Hensley-Clancy, "Stafers, Documents Show Amy Klobuchar's Wrath Toward Her Aides," BuzzFeed News, February 8, 2019, https://www.buzzfeednews.com/article/mollyhensleyclancy/amy-klobuchar-staff-2020-election

[84] Ovunc Kutlu and Gülbin Yildirim, "Obama's Economic Failures Outweigh Successes," Anadolu Agency, November 23, 2016, https://www.aa.com.tr/en/americas/obamas-economic-failures-outweigh-successes/691847

[85] Jennifer Velez, "Michelle Obama Wins Best Spoken Word Album | 2020 GRAMMY's", GRAMMY, January 26, 2020, https://www.grammy.com/grammys/news/michelle-obama-wins-best-spoken-word-album-2020-grammys

86  Caleb Parke. "Sen. Cotton calls out Obama-Biden admin, Clinton on Russia collusion hoax." Fox News. October 7, 2020. https://www.foxnews.com/politics/biden-clinton-obama-trump-russia-collusion-hoax-sen-tom-cotton

87  Andrew Duehren and Dustin Volz, "Hunter Biden's Ukraine Work Raised Concerns With Obama Officials, GOP-Led Probe Confirms," Wall Street Journal, September 23, 2020, https://www.wsj.com/articles/republican-probe-finds-hunter-bidens-ukraine-work-raised-concerns-with-obama-officials-11600859178

88  U.S. Senate Committee on Homeland Security and Governmental Affairs U.S. Senate Committee on Finance Majority Staff, "Hunter Biden, Burisma, and Corruption: The Impact on U.S. Government Policy and Related Concerns," Wall Street Journal, September 23, 2020, https://s.wsj.net/public/resources/documents/HSGAC_Finance_Report_FINAL.pdf

89  U.S. Senate Committee on Homeland Security and Governmental Affairs U.S. Senate Committee on Finance Majority Staff, "Hunter Biden, Burisma, and Corruption: The Impact on U.S. Government Policy and Related Concerns," Wall Street Journal, September 23, 2020, https://s.wsj.net/public/resources/documents/HSGAC_Finance_Report_FINAL.pdf

90  Politifact, "Obameter," Politifact, January 20, 2017, https://www.politifact.com/truth-o-meter/promises/obameter/?ruling=true

91  history.com editors, "Hillary Rodham Clinton," HISTORY, date accessed: June 18, 2021, https://www.history.com/topics/first-ladies/hillary-rodham-clinton

92  Nancy Gibbs and Michael Duffy, "I Misled People," Time, August 31, 1998, http://content.time.com/time/magazine/article/0,9171,988987,00.html

93  Eliza Relman, "These are the sexual-assault allegations against Bill Clinton," Business Insider, June 4, 2018, https://www.businessinsider.com/these-are-the-sexual-assault-allegations-against-bill-clinton-2017-11

94  Matt Drudge, "THE NIGHT HILLARY CLINTON
    MET JUANITA BROADDRICK," Drudge Report, August
    2, 1999, http://www.drudgereportarchives.com/dsp/spe-
    cialReports_pc_carden_detail.htm?reportID=%7B647A-
    4CAA-2DAF-4989-AE48-0AF139FCD3D3%7D

95  Matt Drudge, "THE NIGHT HILLARY CLINTON
    MET JUANITA BROADDRICK," Drudge Report, August
    2, 1999, http://www.drudgereportarchives.com/dsp/spe-
    cialReports_pc_carden_detail.htm?reportID=%7B647A-
    4CAA-2DAF-4989-AE48-0AF139FCD3D3%7D

96  Eliza Relman, "These are the sexual-assault allegations against
    Bill Clinton," Business Insider, June 4, 2018, https://www.busi-
    nessinsider.com/these-are-the-sexual-assault-allegations-against-
    bill-clinton-2017-11

97  Eliza Relman, "These are the sexual-assault allegations against
    Bill Clinton," Business Insider, June 4, 2018, https://www.busi-
    nessinsider.com/these-are-the-sexual-assault-allegations-against-
    bill-clinton-2017-11

98  Rich Lowry, "Yes, Hillary Was an Enabler," Politico
    Magazine, May 26, 2016, https://www.politico.com/magazine/
    story/2016/05/yes-hillary-was-an-enabler-213919

99  Ed Bradley, "Transcript of Interview With Kathleen Willey,"
    The New York Times, March 16, 1998, https://archive.nytimes.
    com/www.nytimes.com/library/politics/031698clinton-wil-
    ley-text.html

100 Pamela Engel, "Former reporter, alleges for the first time that
    Bill Clinton sexually assaulted her decades ago," Business
    Insider, October 19, 2016, https://www.businessinsider.com/
    leslie-millwee-bill-clinton-sexual-assault-2016-10

101 Daniella Diaz, "Trump Calls Clinton 'a nasty woman", CNN,
    October 20, 2016. https://www.cnn.com/2016/10/19/politics/
    donald-trump-hillary-clinton-nasty-woman/index.html

102 "Kendal Clinton Subpoena," The Select House Committee on Benghazi, July 8, 2015, https://archives-benghazi-republicans-oversight.house.gov/sites/republicans.benghazi.house.gov/files/Kendall.Clinton%20Subpoena%20-%202015.03.04.pdf

103 Brooke Singman, "DNI declassifies Brennan notes, CIA memo on Hillary Clinton 'stirring up' scandal between Trump, Russia," Fox News, October 6, 2020, https://www.foxnews.com/politics/dni-brennan-notes-cia-memo-clinton

104 Brooke Singman, "DNI declassifies Brennan notes, CIA memo on Hillary Clinton 'stirring up' scandal between Trump, Russia," Fox News, October 6, 2020, https://www.foxnews.com/politics/dni-brennan-notes-cia-memo-clinton

105 Eli Watkins, "Trump raised 'golden showers thing' with Comey", CNN, April 12, 2018. https://www.cnn.com/2018/04/12/politics/comey-book-golden-showers/index.html

106 Morgan Phillips, "Biden says some funding should 'absolutely' be redirected from police," Fox News, July 8, 2020, https://www.foxnews.com/politics/biden-says-some-funding-should-absolutely-be-redirected-from-police

107 Homes Lybrand, "Fact Check: Biden Falsely Claims he Never Opposed Fracking," CNN, October 23, 2020, https://www.cnn.com/2020/10/23/politics/biden-fracking-fact-check/index.html

108 Ryan Grim, "Joe Biden's Racist Answer on the Legacy of Slavery," the Intercept, September 13, 2019, https://theintercept.com/2019/09/13/joe-biden-democratic-debate-slavery/

109 Robert Longley, "Senator Robert Byrd and the Ku Klux Klan," ThoughtCo., October 30, 2019, https://www.thoughtco.com/robert-byrd-kkk-4147055

110 Adriana Cohen, "Biden's Shocking Tribute to KKK Leader," RealClear Politics, October 2, 2020, https://www.realclearpolitics.com/articles/2020/10/02/bidens_shocking_tribute_to_kkk_leader_144349.html

111 Matt Margolis, "The Top 7 Racist Comments Made by Joe Biden Over the Years", PJMedia, July 23, 2020, https://pjmedia.com/news-and-politics/matt-margolis/2020/07/23/the-top-7-racist-comments-made-by-joe-biden-over-the-years-n673531

112 Matt Margolis, "The Top 7 Racist Comments Made by Joe Biden Over the Years", PJMedia, July 23, 2020, https://pjmedia.com/news-and-politics/matt-margolis/2020/07/23/the-top-7-racist-comments-made-by-joe-biden-over-the-years-n673531

113 Matt Margolis, "The Top 7 Racist Comments Made by Joe Biden Over the Years", PJMedia, July 23, 2020, https://pjmedia.com/news-and-politics/matt-margolis/2020/07/23/the-top-7-racist-comments-made-by-joe-biden-over-the-years-n673531

114 Amanda Prestigiacomo, "8 Women Have Accused Joe Biden of Sexual Misconduct, Inappropriate Touching", the Daily Wire, April 28, 2020, https://www.dailywire.com/news/8-women-have-accused-joe-biden-of-sexual-misconduct-inappropriate-touching

115 U.S. Senate Committee on Homeland Security and Governmental Affairs U.S. Senate Committee on Finance Majority Staff, "Hunter Biden, Burisma, and Corruption: The Impact on U.S. Government Policy and Related Concerns," Wall Street Journal, September 23, 2020, https://s.wsj.net/public/resources/documents/HSGAC_Finance_Report_FINAL.pdf

116 Tim Haines, "FLASHBACK, 2018: Joe Biden Brags At CFR Meeting About Withholding Aid To Ukraine To Force Firing Of Prosecutor", RealClear Politics, September 29, 2019, https://www.realclearpolitics.com/video/2019/09/27/flashback_2018_joe_biden_brags_at_cfr_meeting_about_withholding_aid_to_ukraine_to_force_firing_of_prosecutor.html

117 Baxter Dmitry, "Hunter Biden Text Message To Daughter: 'Unlike Pop, I Won't Make You Give Me Half Your Salary,'" News Punch, October 16, 2020, https://newspunch.com/hunter-biden-text-message-to-daughter-unlike-pop-i-wont-make-you-give-me-half-your-salary/

118 Baxter Dmitry, "Hunter Biden Text Message To Daughter: 'Unlike Pop, I Won't Make You Give Me Half Your Salary,'" News Punch, October 16, 2020, https://newspunch.com/hunter-biden-text-message-to-daughter-unlike-pop-i-wont-make-you-give-me-half-your-salary/

119 Baxter Dmitry, "Hunter Biden Text Message To Daughter: 'Unlike Pop, I Won't Make You Give Me Half Your Salary,'" News Punch, October 16, 2020, https://newspunch.com/hunter-biden-text-message-to-daughter-unlike-pop-i-wont-make-you-give-me-half-your-salary/

120 Adam Shaw, Brooke Singman, "'Plausible deniability': Tony Bobulinski claims Biden family shrugged off concerns about risk to 2020 bid", Fox News, October 27, 2020, https://www.foxnews.com/politics/plausible-deniability-tony-bobulinski-biden-family

121 Adam Shaw, Brooke Singman, "'Plausible deniability': Tony Bobulinski claims Biden family shrugged off concerns about risk to 2020 bid", Fox News, October 27, 2020, https://www.foxnews.com/politics/plausible-deniability-tony-bobulinski-biden-family

122 GianCarlo Canaparo, Hans A. von Spakovski, "Hunter Biden Emails, Texts Raise Questions That Need Answers," The Heritage Foundation, November 2, 2020, https://www.heritage.org/crime-and-justice/commentary/hunter-biden-emails-texts-raise-questions-need-answers

123 Marisa Schultz, "Pelosi on Christopher Columbus Statue Destruction: 'People will do what they do'", Fox News, July 9, 2020. https://www.foxnews.com/politics/pelosi-on-christopher-columbus-statue-destruction-people-will-do-what-they-do

124 "Jussie Smollett: Timeline of the actor's alleged attack and arrest," BBC, February 12, 2020, https://www.bbc.com/news/newsbeat-47317701?intlink_from_url=https://www.bbc.com/news/world/us_and_canada&

125 Christa Marxourals, "Bubba Wallace responds to FBI findings: 'Whether tied in 2019, or whatever, it was a noose'", CNN, June

26, 2020, https://www.cnn.com/2020/06/24/us/bubba-wal-lace-response-fbi-hate-crime-investigation/index.html

126 Lee Brown, "Chicago Black Lives Matter Organizer, Who Called Looting 'reparations' dismisses Peaceful Protesting", Fox News, August 13, 2021. https://www.foxnews.com/us/chi-cago-black-lives-matter-looting-reparations-peaceful-pro-tests-dismissed

127 Christine Tamir, "The Growing Diversity of Black Ameirca", Pew Research Center, March 25, 2021, https://www.pewresearch.org/social-trends/2021/03/25/the-growing-diversity-of-black-america/

128 Emma Colton, "Biden: Administration to make minority and female-owned businesses 'priority,' sparking criti-cisms of 'discrimination,'" Washington Examiner, January 11, 2021, https://www.washingtonexaminer.com/news/biden-minority-female-business-priority

129 Silvia Amaro, "Trump's social media bans are raising new ques-tions on tech regulation," CNBC, January 11, 2020, https://www.cnbc.com/2021/01/11/facebook-twitter-trump-ban-raises-ques-tions-in-uk-and-europe.html

130 Guardian Staff and Agencies, "US congressman who said 'amen and a-woman' prayer hits back at critics", The Guardian, January 5, 2021. https://www.theguardian.com/us-news/2021/jan/05/a-woman-prayer-emanuel-cleaver-amen-critics

131 Daniel Shultz, "The Left Behind: Why Are White American Christians so Racist?", Religion Dispatch, August 5, 2020, https://religiondispatches.org/the-left-behind-why-are-white-american-christians-so-racist/

132 Daniel Shultz, "The Left Behind: Why Are White American Christians so Racist?", Religion Dispatch, August 5, 2020, https://religiondispatches.org/the-left-behind-why-are-white-american-christians-so-racist/

133  Daniel Shultz, "The Left Behind: Why Are White
     American Christians so Racist?", Religion Dispatch,
     August 5, 2020, https://religiondispatches.org/
     the-left-behind-why-are-white-american-christians-so-racist/

134  Daniel Shultz, "The Left Behind: Why Are White
     American Christians so Racist?", Religion Dispatch,
     August 5, 2020, https://religiondispatches.org/
     the-left-behind-why-are-white-american-christians-so-racist/

135  Zouhair Mazouz, "Getting It Wrong About Islam: Check
     Your Secular Privilege, Liberal America," wbur, December
     1, 2016, https://www.wbur.org/cognoscenti/2016/12/01/
     liberals-islam-zouhair-mazouz

136  Jon Macks, "Donald Trump: God's Gift to Comedy," CNN, July
     14, 2015, https://www.cnn.com/2015/07/14/opinions/macks-
     comics-love-trump/index.html

137  Jon Macks, "Donald Trump: God's Gift to Comedy," CNN, July
     14, 2015, https://www.cnn.com/2015/07/14/opinions/macks-
     comics-love-trump/index.html

138  Timothy Stanley, "Donald Trump can win-and he must
     be stopped," CNN, February 11, 2016, https://www.cnn.
     com/2016/02/10/opinions/donald-trump-republican-par-
     ty-stanley/index.html

CPSIA information can be obtained
at www.ICGtesting.com
Printed in the USA
BVHW070948221221
624594BV00012B/1137

9 781662 835209